THE VICTORIA AND ALBERT MUSEUM

Introduction by the Director

The Victoria and Albert Museum

Text by the Curators

SCALA BOOKS
Published in association with
The Victoria and Albert Museum

© 1991 Scala Publications Ltd

First published 1991
by Scala Publications Ltd
3 Greek Street
London W1V 6NX

Distributed in the USA and Canada by
Rizzoli International Publications, Inc
300 Park Avenue South
New York
NY 10010

Special assistance within museum by Elizabeth James
Designed by Alan Bartram
Edited by Paul Holberton
Produced by Scala Publications Ltd
Filmset by August Filmsetting, Haydock, St Helens, England
Printed and bound by Graphicom, Vicenza, Italy

ISBN 1 870248 67 8

Contents

Introduction

The Victoria and Albert Museum is a monument to the cultural ideals of mid-Victorian England. The first of these ideals was the desire to influence the standards of design in British manufactures; the second was to make available works of art on public display to the working population; the third to use the Museum as an instrument in the education of public taste.

During the 1830s the government had been worried by the extent to which the sales of high-class goods were dominated by French imports. In 1835, a Select Committee of Arts and Manufactures was appointed 'to enquire into the best means of extending a knowledge of the ARTS and the PRINCIPLES of DESIGN among the People (especially the Manufacturing Population) of the country; also to inquire into the constitution, management and effects of Institutions concerned with the Arts'. In 1836, the committee recommended both that schools of design should be established and that the government should set up public museums. As Dr Waagen, the Director of the Berlin Museum, made clear in his evidence to the committee:

By giving the people an opportunity of seeing the most beautiful objects of art in the particular branch which they follow; by having collections of the most beautiful models of furniture and of different objects of manufacture. It is not enough merely to form these collections; there must be instructions to teach people on what principles those models have been formed; furthermore, for the purpose of exercising the hand and eye, it is useful that young people should draw and model after those models.

In 1837, a School of Design in Ornamental Art at Somerset House was established and it soon began to collect examples of contemporary art for purposes of instruction; but the establishment of a Museum of ornamental art had to wait until 1852, when, following the Great Exhibition, a Museum of Manufactures opened at Marlborough House, with Henry Cole, a prominent public servant and the brains behind the Great Exhibition, as General Superintendent and John Charles Robinson, a connoisseur of medieval and Renaissance art, as superintendent of the art collections. In his first annual report to the Board of Trade, Cole outlined his belief that:

a Museum presents probably the only effectual means of educating the adult, who cannot be expected to go to school like the youth, and the necessity for teaching the grown man is quite as great as that of training the child. By proper arrangements a Museum may be made in the highest degree instructional. If it be connected with lectures, and means are taken to point out its uses and applications, it becomes elevated from being a mere unintelligible lounge for idlers into an impressive schoolroom for everyone.

Almost as soon as the Museum had been established, it began to acquire important collections, including, in 1855, the Gherardini collection of models for sculpture and items from the Bernal collection of majolica and, in 1856, the Soulages collection of Renaissance applied arts; but it is important to be aware, in understanding the history of the Museum, that its educational and didactic purposes preceded the acquisition of its collections. It was to be a distinctive type of Museum, oriented towards the understanding and interpretation of the principles of design in manufactured goods, educational in the ways that the collections were displayed, and to be enjoyed by as broad an audience as possible.

Since the Museum was established, it has pursued these ideals, not always with equal success. At the heart of the Museum and central to its activities are the collections of three-dimensional design: furniture and woodwork, textiles and dress, metalwork, and ceramics and glass. These collections were established in order to demonstrate changes in design practice within a particular material, following the precepts of Gottfried Semper, the mid-nineteenth-century design theorist who believed in the primacy of particular materials, textiles, ceramics, carpentry and stone, in the origins of architectural form. The major part of these collections is on display in the galleries, mostly on the upper floors of the Museum, which used to be known as the study galleries, but have recently been renamed the Materials and Techniques Galleries. The works in the galleries are supported by study facilities, which are available on request to students; not all the works in the collection can be displayed, either because of constraints of space (in which case they are often loaned to other public collections) or of conservation.

Alongside the major collections of three-dimensional design is the Collection of Prints, Drawings and Paintings, housed in the Henry Cole Wing. Part of the purpose of this collection is to document the design process, so it includes substantial holdings of prints, which were a source of inspiration to designers, and of drawings, which record how objects were conceived; but it also includes major collections of paintings (in 1856, John Sheepshanks, a wealthy Yorkshire cloth manufacturer, donated his British paintings by Etty, Landseer, Stanfield, Naysmyth and Constable in order to form a National Gallery of British Art alongside the Museum of Manufactures) and of photographs, in the study of which the Museum has been a pioneer.

The presence of paintings alongside works of applied art and design indicates the extent to which it was believed that art and design were intimately associated. Fine art was to be source of inspiration to designers and manufacturers. So, as well as being one of the world's great Museums of applied art, the V&A also houses the National collection of sculpture. Indeed, to the casual visitor, the collections of sculpture are more evident than the other holdings, partly because of their great scale, partly because they occupy the galleries closest to the main entrance, and partly because they include some of the most important individual masterpieces, including Donatello's *Ascension with Christ giving the Keys to St Peter*, Bernini's *Neptune*, and Roubiliac's wonderful statue of *George Frederick Handel*, which was first on public display in the mid-eighteenth-century Vauxhall gardens.

Since its foundation in 1852, the so called Museum of Manufactures has changed its name, in 1857 to the South Kensington Museum, and then, when Queen Victoria laid the foundation stone of the new building in 1899, to the Victoria and Albert Museum, in memory of the significant rôle Prince Albert had played in its foundation. It has shed some of its collections, including animal and food products and marine models; and it has acquired additional Museums to supplement its central holdings.

Of these additional Museums, the first was the Museum at Bethnal Green, which consisted of the bulk of the original Museum buildings, the so-called 'Brompton Boilers', transferred by sappers to the East End, clad in brick, and opened in 1872. After the First World War the Bethnal Green Museum became a microcosm of the main Museum at South Kensington, with a range of displays which included the Donaldson gift of Art Nouveau furniture acquired at the 1900 Paris Exhibition and a special focus on local industries – furniture, shoes, and Spitalfields silks; but, in 1975, it was decided to make the Bethnal Green Museum into a Museum of Childhood, concentrating on the study of toys, dolls, childrens' books and games.

In 1874, the former collections of the East India Company, transferred to Crown ownership in 1858, were moved to South Kensington, where they have always been displayed independently of the main collections; and the principle of studying Asian culture separately from the traditions of European design was extended to the East Asian collections in 1970, when a Far Eastern Department was established, thereby allowing staff to learn the languages required for the study of the original context of the objects in their care.

Most recent of the additional Museums attached to the main Museum in South Kensington is the Theatre Museum. The idea that there should be a theatre Museum in England, as there is in a number of European countries, has been around since at least 1871, when the actor Henry Neville suggested that there should be 'a Burlington House of the theatre'. Then in 1911 Gabrielle Enthoven, who had made an important collection of theatrical materials, embarked on a long campaign to find it an appropriate home. In 1924 it was acquired by the V&A and run under the auspices of the Department of Engraving, Illustration and Design. Gradually pressure built up to establish it as an independent entity and, in 1974, the Theatre Museum was established, incorporating not only the Enthoven collection, but also the holdings of the Harry R. Beard theatre collection and the former British Theatre Museum. In 1975, a site for the Museum was acquired in the Flower Market in Covent Garden and the Theatre Museum was eventually opened in its own specially converted premises on 23 April 1987.

Since the Second World War, the main developments in South Kensington have involved not only the addition of new responsibilities, but also changes in the ways the collections have been conserved, interpreted and displayed. After the War, the then Director, Leigh Ashton, decided that it was essential to establish a set of galleries which would attract the general public; and that the way to do this was to have so called primary galleries which would consist of the most important works of art of a particular historical period. As laid out in the 1950s, these galleries were deliberately didactic, with large instructional panels, making clear changes in the general history of design, style, patronage, and taste. More recently, these galleries have been redesignated 'Art and Design Galleries' and much of the energy of the institution is dedicated towards raising funds so that they can be kept up to date in their methods of presentation.

In 1960, a Department of Conservation was established and one of the major developments in Museum practice over the last three decades has been the change from a view of conservation as a technical expertise involving the repair and refurbishment of works of art to conservation as a science necessarily involving the control of conditions of display and storage. The Conservation department now has a national rôle in the development of conservation practice, is substantially involved in research and training, and has well over 50 people working on the care of the collections.

The next major development in the Museum was the establishment of a separate education section responsible for the organization of programmes for schools. Although the Museum had always been conceived as a vehicle for the instruction of public taste, its main audience has traditionally consisted of academic scholars, who are interested in the historical development of the applied arts; students in art colleges, who are learning about the antecedents of their discipline; collectors, who have used the Museum as a resource for the study of comparative examples; and connoisseurs who have come to enjoy and appreciate the range of works of art on display. Since the 1960s, an emphasis has been placed on trying to make the collections accessible to a broader audience, which should include school children and adults who are learning for the first time about a subject, which they may initially find at least unfamiliar and possibly alien. In this way the Museum has tried to recover its original didactic purposes.

The third area of development since the Second World War has been in the policy of holding temporary exhibitions. There have been exhibitions of one sort or another in the Museum ever since it opened, including, for example, an exhibition of Spanish Art Treasures in 1881, which attracted more than a million visitors, exhibitions in the 1930s commemorating the bicentenary of Josiah Wedgwood and the centenary of William Morris, the 'Britain Can Make It' exhibition in 1946 and a pioneering exhibition of Victorian and Edwardian decorative arts held in 1952. In the 1960s big exhibitions became an increasingly important vehicle for communicating ideas about specialist areas in the history of art, and for attracting new audiences into museums. Notable exhibitions held while Sir John Pope-Hennessy was Director included the life and works of Charles Dickens (many of whose manuscripts are held by the National Art Library, a department of the Museum) in 1970, Victorian Church Art in 1971, and the mammoth Council of Europe exhibition 'The Age of Neo-Classicism' which was shown in sites all over London in 1972. Under Sir Roy Strong, exhibitions at the V&A became an art form: they included 'The Destruction of the Country House' in 1975, Fabergé in 1977, and 'Rococo: Art and Design in Hogarth's England' in 1984. More recently our policy has been to concentrate on the development of the north and south courts of the Museum, which, from autumn 1991, will make available one of the largest arenas for exhibitions in London, providing us with the opportunity for developing further the diverse possibilities of exhibition display.

Any account of the history of the Museum demonstrates the extent to which its formation has been a combination of idealism and pragmatism. Its current form is as much the result of a long historical process as it is a model of internal logic. Indeed, the strength of the V&A as an institution is precisely its capaciousness. It is a Museum both of fine art and of design. It incorporates elements of an aesthetic canon and a more broad-ranging documentation of material and craft practices. It would be possible to strip the Museum back to its original form, as a museum only of three-dimensional design or, as it is boldly described over the pediment of the original courtyard building, THE FIRST EXHIBITION OF THE WORKS OF INDUSTRY OF ALL NATIONS.

But the Museum is itself now a monument to changing government policies and aesthetic ideas. It is a highly complex synthesis of cultural aspirations representing more than a century of collecting in an enormous variety of fields. It is important to temper idealism in defining the purposes of the Museum with a degree of pragmatism about its operation. At no point in its history has it been monolithic in the way that it has operated. It has always been subject to intense conflicts about its appropriate rôle. Rather than worrying about this, it is better to embrace the protean aspect of what is by any standards a great national and public institution.

Recently the Museum has embarked on a major policy of reorganization, which has attempted to clarify its diverse functions. It now consists of two major divisions, Collections and Administration; within the Administration division, there are departments of Conservation, Collections, Research, and the National Art Library; and within the Collections Department, there are the following Collections – Ceramics and Glass; Far Eastern; Furniture and Woodwork; Indian and South-East Asian; Metalwork; Prints, Drawings, and Paintings; Sculpture; and Textiles and Dress. It is my task to ensure that the energies of the Museum and its staff are directed towards acquiring works of art and design as systematically and representatively as possible; towards ensuring that they are kept in appropriate conditions and are available for purposes of study; towards developing the scholarship which sustains the understanding and interpretation of art and design; and, perhaps above all, towards improving the methods of communication which make the Museum available to as large an audience as possible.

ELIZABETH ESTEVE-COLL
Director
May 1991

The Sculpture Collections

The Museum contains the National Collection of European post-classical sculpture, spanning the period from Early Christian times to about 1914; the major holdings of twentieth-century sculpture are housed in the Tate Gallery.

The collection of medieval ivories is one of the greatest in the world, in terms of both quality and size. It includes pieces from late antiquity such as the Roman Symmachi panel, dating from about AD 400, and remarkable early medieval and Byzantine works such as the Holy Water bucket made in Milan in the late tenth century (known as the Basilewsky *situla*), and the so called Veroli casket, made in Constantinople in the late tenth or early eleventh century. The great period of French ivory carving in the thirteenth and fourteenth centuries is represented by exquisite statuettes of the *Virgin and Child*, and by secular mirror-backs, decorated with scenes of courtly chivalry. The Baroque ivories include pieces from France, Germany, England and the Spanish and Portuguese colonies in Latin America and Goa. The works of French ivory-carvers active in England, such as David Le Marchand and Jean Cavalier, are especially notable, as they exemplify virtuoso skills in portraiture and figurative carving on a small scale.

The collection of Italian sculpture is unparalleled outside Italy. Giovanni Pisano's prophet *Haggai*, formerly on the façade of Siena Cathedral, dominates Room 22, devoted to Italian Gothic art, and around the quadrangle are displayed works by Donatello, Ghiberti, Desiderio da Settignano, Antonio Rossellino, the della Robbia family, and other Renaissance masters. Sixteenth-century Italy is represented by the small marble figures and reliefs, often of mythological subjects, by the North Italian sculptors Antonio Lombardo and Agostino Busti, known as Bambaia. Some of the finest Renaissance bronzes are those of Antico and Riccio; Antico's courtly style is epitomised by his *Meleager*, while the rich surface of Riccio's *Shouting horseman* illustrates the liveliness of his approach. One of the most treasured objects in the collection is the wax study of a *Slave* by Michelangelo, a preliminary model for one of the figures planned for the tomb of Pope Julius II in Rome.

On a large scale, Giambologna's great *Samson and the Philistine* is rivalled only by Bernini's *Neptune and a Triton*: both were originally fountain figures. Other works by these sculptors in bronze, wax and terracotta illustrate the full range of their achievements. Contemporary works by Algardi, Foggini and others further show the wealth of sculptural production at this time.

The medals held at the Museum are of high quality: fifteenth-century works by Pisanello, Adriano Fiorentino and other Italian medallists, along with German medals and wood models of the sixteenth century, demonstrate the start of the tradition; later Italian, French, Flemish and English medals show the evolution of medallic art.

In the early sixteenth century, much of the wood sculpture made in Germany and the Netherlands was for large altarpieces; also typical of this period were small statuettes and reliefs for private collectors, which could be secular or for devotional purposes. The limewood figures of *Mary Salome and Zebedee* by Tilman Riemenschneider of Würzburg were once part of an altarpiece, while the minutely carved boxwood *Virgin and Child* by the Nuremberg artist Veit Stoss was probably made for a domestic setting. Amongst the Spanish wood sculpture, the figure of a saint by the sixteenth-century artist Alonso Berruguete, and the *Virgin of Sorrows* by the seventeenth-century Pedro de Mena, are particularly noteworthy.

English sculpture is naturally well represented, from the largest collection of medieval alabaster carvings in the world (acquired mainly through the generosity of the donor Dr W. L. Hildburgh), to the comprehensive display of marble and stone monuments, busts and figures, most of which can be seen in Room 50. Outstanding both in scale and innovation is Roubiliac's statue of the musician *Handel*, balanced on the other side of the gallery by Rysbrack's seated Saxon god *Thuner* from Stowe. Of the nineteenth-century works, Alfred Stevens's models for the Duke of Wellington's tomb in Westminster Abbey command attention.

Works by Houdon and Clodion from the eighteenth century, and by Carpeaux and Dalou from the nineteenth century, are some of the highlights of the later French sculpture. A large group of the Rodin bronzes was donated by the artist in 1914, and is therefore especially valued.

The vast collection of plaster casts housed in the Cast Courts are reproductions (mostly made in the nineteenth century) of major works from Italy, Spain and northern Europe, and include Michelangelo's *David* and the Portico de la Gloria from the Cathedral at Santiago de Compostela.

1

2

1
Carolingian (Aachen), *c*810
The front cover of the Lorsch Gospels
Ivory, height 38.1 cm, width 26.7 cm
Inv.no.138-1866
The back cover, now in the Vatican
Museums in Rome, shows Christ
between two archangels, with two
flying angels above holding a
medallion with a cross, and below, the
Magi before Herod and the Adoration
of the Magi.

2
**Anglo-Saxon, *c*1000 (back and sides
German (?), 10th century)**
Reliquary cross,
height 18.5 cm, width 13.4 cm
Inv.no.7943-1862.
Gold plaques on a cedar base, the
figure of Christ in walrus ivory, the
inscription and medallions depicting
the symbols of the Evangelists in
cloisonné enamel.

3
Roman, *c*400
Leaf of a diptych (The Symmachi
panel)
Ivory, height 29.5 cm, width 12 cm
Inv.no.212-1865
The other half of this diptych is now
in the Cluny Museum in Paris. The
diptych was made to commemorate
some kind of alliance between two
notable families of 4th-century Rome,
the Symmachi and the Nicomachi.

4

5

6

4
Ottonian (Milan), *c*980
The Basilewsky *situla*
Ivory, height 16 cm
Inv.no.A18-1933
This *situla* or Holy Water bucket bears
twelve scenes from the Passion of
Christ. Ivory Holy Water buckets are
extremely rare, only four being
known.

5
Byzantine, 12th century
*St John the Baptist and four saints (Philip,
Stephen, Thomas and Andrew)*
Ivory, height 23.5 cm, width 13.5 cm
Inv.no.215-1866

6
**Hispano-Arabic (Cordoba), early
11th century**
Casket
Ivory with later silver mounts,
height 21.6 cm, length 26.7 cm,
width 16.2 cm
Inv.no.10-1866

1
English (Winchester?), *c*1150-70
Head of a crozier
Ivory, height 12 cm, width 11 cm
Inv.no.218-1865
The crozier shows three scenes relating to the Infancy of Christ and a further three devoted to the life of St Nicholas; it is probable, therefore, that it was made for an institution dedicated to that saint, or for an abbot or bishop of the same name.

1

2

2
Spanish, *c*1135-50
The Adoration of the Magi
Whalebone, height 36.5 cm, width (at base) 16 cm
Inv.no.142-1866

3
English, *c*1180
Lectern
Limestone ('Wenlock marble'), height 31 cm, width 58 cm, depth 59 cm
Inv.no.A21-1984
This lectern or reading desk was supported by a square capital and column or pillar, but these have not survived. It is one of only three 12th-century lecterns in England, the others being at Norton and Crowle (Worcestershire).

3

4

4
Byzantine (Constantinople), 10th-11th century
The Veroli casket
Ivory and bone on wood, height 11.5 cm, length 40.5 cm, width 15.5 cm
Inv.no.216-1865
This casket, formerly in the cathedral treasury at Veroli (south-east of Rome), shows scenes from classical mythology. The casket may have belonged to a person close to the imperial court, and was perhaps used to hold scent bottles or jewellery.

5
French (Paris), early 14th century
The Virgin and Child
Ivory, height 36 cm
Inv.no.4685-1858

6
Arnolfo di Cambio (c1245-1302?)
Italian (Florence)
The Annunciation, about 1300

Marble, height 74.5 cm, width 128 cm
Said to come from the church of Santa
Croce, Florence; inv.no.7563-1861
The Virgin is closely related to
Arnolfo's style when he was working
in Rome at the end of the 13th
century, and the *Annunciation* on the
outside of the Duomo at Florence
(about 1310) derives from the present
relief.

5

4

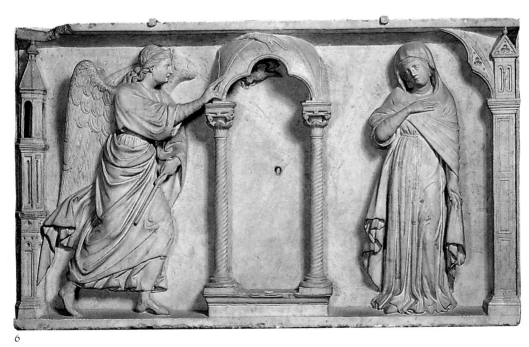
6

13

1
French (Ile-de-France), c1340-50
The Virgin and Child
Limestone, painted and gilded, height
173 cm
Inv.no.A98-1911; gift of J. Pierpont
Morgan

2
Giovanni Pisano (c1250-after 1314)
Italian (Pisa)
The Crucified Christ, about 1300
Ivory, with traces of pigmentation,
height 15 cm
Inv.no.212-1867

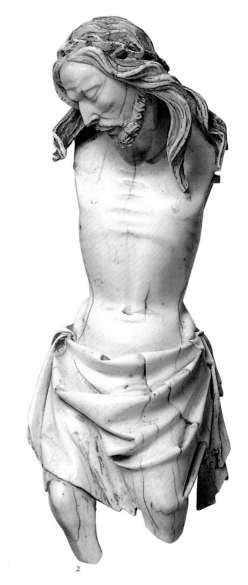

2

1

3
Southern Netherlandish, *c*1430
The Virgin with the dead Christ
Alabaster, height 38.4 cm, width (of base) 31 cm
Inv.no.A28-1960; gift of Sir Thomas Barlow
This small *Pietà* group is attributed to the so called 'Master of Rimini', a Southern Netherlandish craftsman whose work was exported to north-east Italy amongst other places. His most famous work, an altarpiece once in a church in Rimini, is now in the Liebieghaus Museum in Frankfurt.

4
Bartolommeo Buon (*c*1374-1467?)
Italian (Venice)
The Virgin and Child with kneeling members of the Guild of the Misericordia, about 1445-50
Istrian stone, height 251.5 cm, width 208.3 cm

From the Scuola Vecchia della Misericordia, Venice; inv.no.25-1882
The relief was carved for the tympanum over the principal doorway of the Scuola. It was bought in 1882 from the Misericordia when the church was in disrepair, in order to preserve it.

4

15

1
Donatello (c1386-1466)
Italian (Florence)
The Ascension of Christ with the Giving of the Keys to St Peter, c1430 (detail)
Marble, height 40.6 cm, width 114.3 cm
Inv.no.7629-1861
The relief is a fine example of Donatello's low, *stiacciato* (literally 'squashed') relief. It is possible that the relief was originally intended to be placed under a statue on Orsanmichele, Florence, in a similar manner to the artist's relief of *St George and the dragon.*

2
Agostino di Duccio (1418-81)
Italian (Florence)
Virgin and Child with five angels, mid-15th century
Marble, height 55.9 cm, width 47.9 cm
Inv.no.A14-1926; purchased with the assistance of the National Art Collections Fund and Lord Duveen of Millbank
The style of the relief relates to Agostino's work at the Tempio Malatestiano at Rimini, about 1454, and it is probable that the relief was carved in Rimini at around this date.

3
Antonio Rossellino (1427-79)
Italian (Florence)
Giovanni Chellini, 1456
Marble, height 51.1 cm
Inv.no.7671-1861
The bust, which is signed and dated underneath, was made from a life mask of the well-known Florentine doctor when he was about 77 years old.

4
Donatello (c1386-1466)
Italian (Florence)
The Virgin and Child with Four Angels (The Chellini *Madonna*), 1456
Bronze with traces of gilding, diameter 28.5 cm
Inv.no.A1-1976; purchased with the aid of public subscription, with donations from the National Art Collections Fund and the Pilgrim Trust in memory of David, Earl of Crawford and Balcarres
The reverse of the roundel is a negative cast of the relief, forming a mould from which glass copies can be made. It was a gift from the artist to Dr Giovanni Chellini in thanks for medical treatment he had received, in the same year as Rossellino carved the doctor's bust.

5
Antonio Rossellino (1427-79)
Italian (Florence)
The Madonna and Child, c1465
Terracotta, height 48.3 cm
Inv.no.4495-1858
The statuette, known as *The Virgin with the laughing Child,* was probably a sketch model for a larger work. The style and drapery forms are related to the angels on the tomb of the Cardinal of Portugal by Rossellino in San Miniato al Monte, Florence.

1

2

3

6

Andrea del Verrocchio (1435-88)
Italian (Florence)
Sketch-model for a monument to
Cardinal Niccolò Forteguerri, c1476
Terracotta, height 39.4 cm, width
26.7 cm
Inv.no.7599-1861

4

5

6

1

South German, c1500-20
Palmesel (Christ entering Jerusalem)
Painted limewood, height 147.2 cm
Inv.no.1030-1910; Murray bequest
This wood sculpture was originally
mounted on wheels, and would have
been taken through the streets in
procession on Palm Sunday.

2

**Agostino Busti, called Bambaia
(1483-1548)**
Italian (Milan)
Youth leading a rearing horse, c1500-25
Marble, height 41.3 cm, width 36.4 cm
Inv.no.7260-1860
The relief (together with two others in
the collection and one in the Prado,
Madrid) appears to have formed part
of a secular decorative scheme, which
was probably never completed.

3

**Andrea Briosco, called Il Riccio
(c.1470-1532)**
Italian (Padua)
Satyr and Satyress, about 1507
Bronze, height (including base)
27.5 cm
Inv.no.A.8-1949; given by the
National Art Collections Fund.
Satyrs and satyresses were favourite
subjects of Riccio's workshop and are
characteristic of the artist's humanist
environment. This group is roughly
contemporary with his greatest work,
the huge candlestick in the Santo at
Padua, begun in 1507.

4

**Pier Jacopo Alari-Bonacolsi, called
Antico (c1460-1528)**
Italian (Mantua)
Meleager, late 15th century
Bronze, parcel-gilt and inlaid with
silver, height 32.1 cm
Inv.no.A27-1960; purchased with
contributions from the Horn and
Bryan bequests and with the
assistance of the National Art
Collections Fund
The classical marble statue on which
the statuette is based was popularly
known as 'the peasant'. This bronze
appears to be identical with 'a metal
figure of a peasant' known to have
belonged to Gianfrancesco Gonzaga
(1446-96), Lord of Rodrigo.

1

2

3

4

5

5
Andrea della Robbia (1435-1525)
Italian (Florence)
The Adoration of the Magi, early 16th
century
Polychrome tin-glazed terracotta,
height 222.3 cm, width 175.3 cm
Inv.no.4412-1857

The appearance of the Albizzi arms on
the predella suggests that the
altarpiece may have been
commissioned for one of the churches
under their patronage. The
composition is closely related to an
altarpiece by Perugino (Perugia,
Pinacoteca Nazionale).

1
Veit Stoss (c1447-1533)
German (Nuremberg)
The Virgin and Child, c1480
Boxwood, height 20.3 cm
Inv.no.646-1893
This small figure group illustrates the
virtuosity of Stoss's carving. Remains
of gilding survive on the edges of the
Virgin's cloak and veil.

2
Tilman Riemenschneider
(c1460-1531)
German (Würzburg)
Mary Salome and Zebedee, c1520
Limewood, glazed, 119.4 × 49.5 cm
Inv.no.110-1878

According to the apocryphal legends
Mary Salome was the Virgin Mary's
half-sister, and Zebedee was her
husband. These figures come from a
larger altarpiece which showed other
members of Christ's family.

1

2

3

French (Troyes), c1525
Altarpiece of the Annunciation and
the Passion of Christ
Limestone, painted and gilded, height
186.7 cm, width 86.4 cm (central
section), each wing height 77.5 cm,
width 91.4 cm
Inv.no.4413-1857
This altarpiece came originally from
the collegiate church at Lirey, near
Troyes. The donor, who kneels in the
robes of a canon in the foreground of
the Crucifixion scene, was Jean
Huyard 'l'Ainé' (died 1541). His coat-
of-arms appears in the pendentive
between the two left-hand arches.

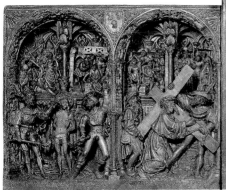

3

3

1

Jacopo Sansovino (1486-1570)
Italian (Florence)
The Descent from the Cross, c1510
Gilt wax and wood, height 76.2 cm,
width 72.4 cm (relief only)
Inv.no.7595-1861

This model was made for the painter
Perugino when Sansovino was in
Rome between 1506 and 1511.
Several related paintings survive,
which all depend from a lost original
by Perugino.

1

2

3

4

22

2
**Michelangelo Buonarroti
(1475-1564)**
Italian (Florence)
Study for a *Slave*, c1516
Red wax, height 16.7 cm
Inv.no.4117-1854
This is a sketch model for the
unfinished, marble figure of the young
Slave (Accademia, Florence), designed
for the 1516 scheme of the tomb of
Pope Julius II in San Pietro in Vincoli,
Rome.

3
Benvenuto Cellini (1500-71)
Italian (Florence)
Head of Medusa, about 1550
Bronze, height 13.9 cm
Inv.no.A14-1964
The model is a study of the head of
Medusa for the statue of Perseus in
the Loggia dei Lanzi, Florence. Cellini
describes the casting process for the
statue in his famous *Autobiography*.

4
Pietro Torrigiano (1472-1528)
Italian (Florence), active in England
King Henry VII, c1509-11
Painted and gilded terracotta, height
60.6 cm
Inv.no.A49-1935; purchased by the
John Webb Trust
The bust was made using a death
mask, fleshed out to produce life-like
features. Torrigiano was also
responsible for Henry's gilt bronze
tomb in his funerary chapel at
Westminster Abbey.

5
Giovanni Bologna (1529-1608)
Italo-Flemish, active in Florence
Samson slaying a Philistine, c1562
Marble, height 209.9 cm
Inv.no.A7-1954; purchased with the
assistance of the National Art
Collections Fund
This sculpture is the earliest of
Giambologna's great marble groups.
Commissioned by Francesco de'
Medici, it subsequently surmounted a
fountain in Florence which was then
given to a Spanish duke in Valladolid.
The group came to England from
Spain in 1623, having been presented
to King Charles I (then Prince of
Wales).

5

1
Adriaen de Fries (c1545-1626)
North Netherlandish
Emperor Rudolph II, signed and dated
1609
Bronze, height 71.1 cm, width 34.9 cm
Inv.no.6920-1860
De Fries trained in Giambologna's
workshop in Florence before working
at Augsburg and becoming court
sculptor at Prague in 1601. This is the
last of three relief portraits of the
Holy Roman Emperor by the artist.

2
**Giovanni Lorenzo Bernini
(1598-1680)**
Italian (Rome)
Thomas Baker (1606-1658), c1638
Marble, height 81.6 cm
Inv.no.A63-1921
Thomas Baker was an English
gentleman who travelled extensively
in Europe before becoming High
Sheriff of Suffolk in 1657. He
commissioned this bust after visiting
Bernini's studio in Rome in 1636 to
see a bust of King Charles I.

1

2

3
Alessandro Algardi (1595-1654)
Italian (Rome)
Cardinal Paolo Emilio Zacchia c1650
Terracotta, height 82.2 cm, width
82.9 cm
Inv.no.A78-1970; purchased with the
assistance of the National Art
Collections Fund and a contribution
from the Horn bequest
This sketch model was made in
preparation for a marble bust which
remained unfinished at the artist's
death. The liveliness of the portrait is
remarkable as it was modelled
posthumously; the sitter had died
nearly fifty years earlier.

3

Giovanni Lorenzo Bernini (1598-1680)
Italian (Rome)
Neptune and Triton, c1622
Marble, height 182.2 cm
Inv.no.A18-1950; purchased with the
assistance of the National Art
Collections Fund and with

contributions from the John Webb
Trust and the Vallentin bequest
This fountain group is an early work
by Bernini, commissioned by Cardinal
Montalto for his villa in Rome.
Amongst the subsequent owners was
Sir Joshua Reynolds, who brought the
sculpture to England in 1787.

1

Michael Rysbrack (1694-1770)
Flemish, active in England
The architect James Gibbs (1682-1754),
1726
Marble, signed and dated, height
67.2 cm with socle
Inv.no.A6-1988; purchased with
contributions from the National
Heritage Memorial Fund and the
National Art Collections Fund
(Eugene Cremetti Fund)
Gibbs was the outstanding architect of
the early 18th century, and a close
associate of Rysbrack, who carried out
work for him. This bust is possibly the
one recorded in Horace Walpole's
collection at Strawberry Hill, and was
purchased by the Museum from the
church of St Martin-in-the-Fields,
which Gibbs designed.

2

3

2
Pedro de Mena (1628-88)
Spanish
The Sorrowing Virgin, c1650
Painted wood and ivory, height
42.5 cm
Inv.no.1284-1871
This devotional piece was probably
set on an altar. Other versions by the
artist survive in Spain and elsewhere,
but this is a particularly fine example,
the eyes being made of painted ivory.

3
Hubert Le Sueur (1595?-1650)
French, active in England
Charles I of England, 1631
Marble, signed, height 87.6 cm
Inv.no.A35-1910
This bust was probably placed in the
garden of St James's Palace. Le Sueur
usually worked in bronze; this rare
marble may have been a royal
commission.

4
**Louis-François Roubiliac
(1705?-1762)**
French, active in England
George Frederick Handel (1685-1759),
1738
Marble, signed, height 135 cm
Inv.no.A3-1965; purchased with the
assistance of the National Art
Collections Fund
This full-length statue of Handel
originally stood in Vauxhall Gardens.
It is the earliest known life-size
representation in marble of a living
artist, who is portrayed sitting relaxed
and dressed informally, while holding
the lyre of Apollo, or possibly
Orpheus.

1
Clodion (Claude Michel)
(1738-1814)
French
Cupid and Psyche, c1780
Terracotta, height 59 cm
Inv.no.A23-1958; given by Sir Chester
Beatty
Clodion specialised in terracotta, and
his subtle handling of the material is
epitomised in this sensuous group.

2
Antonio Canova (1769-1882)
Italian
Theseus and the Minotaur, 1782
Marble, height 145.4 cm
Inv.no.A5-1962; purchased with the
assistance of the National Art
Collections Fund

Canova sculpted this marble in Rome
at the age of 24. Theseus is portrayed
after he has slain the Minotaur;
apparently Canova was advised that
his reputation would gain more from a
static group than from one showing
violent movement.

1

2

3
Antoine-Louis Barye (1796-1875)
French (Paris)
Running Elephant of Senegal, c1880
(model c1865)
Bronze, height 14 cm, length 19 cm
Inv.no.62-1882.S.EX.
Barye was the leading *'animalier'*
sculptor, producing many small
bronzes of animals from around 1830
onwards. This one was actually cast
just after his death in 1875, as it bears
the stamp of the Barbédienne foundry
in Paris, who took over the artist's
models in that year.

4
John Flaxman (1755-1826)
English
St Michael overcoming Satan, 1822
Plaster, height 77.8 cm
Inv.no.312-1898
This is the original plaster model for
the group in marble at Petworth
House; it is one of Flaxman's last
works.

3

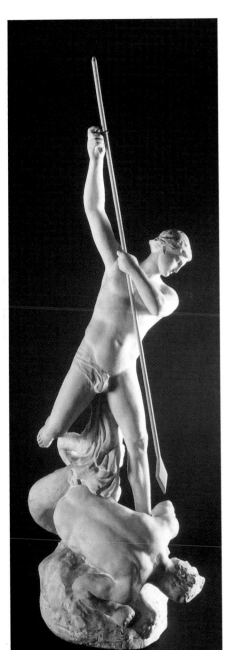

Leon Underwood (1891-1977)
English
Mindslave, 1934
Marble, height 112 cm
Inv.no.A1-1981
Underwood attempted to convey in
this piece something of the mental
repression experienced in central
Europe in the early 1930s.

4

5

7

5

Auguste Rodin (1840-1917)
French
St John the Baptist, 1880
Bronze, height 200 cm
Inv.no.601-1902
This is a cast of one of Rodin's earliest
successful works, and was purchased
by public subscription in 1902. It was
the first work by Rodin to enter an
English public collection.

6

Aimé-Jules Dalou (1838-1902)
French, active in England
Bacchanales, 1879
Terracotta, diameter 175 cm
Inv.no.434-1896
This work was exhibited at the Royal
Academy in 1879.

6

The Pictorial Collections

The Victoria and Albert Museum is known internationally as a great museum of the decorative arts, yet also possesses many paintings, numerically even more than the National Gallery. The explanation for this lies in the early guidelines on collecting policy. They were once summarised by its patron the Prince Consort as the acquisition of objects which would 'improve the standards of taste and manufacture by providing constant reference to the best examples of the decorative and fine arts of the past'. As a result of later interpretations of these aims, the Museum's present collections are unique in their range and eclecticism. Under one roof – the Print Room – the visitor can now not only study designs for arms and armour, ceramics, furniture, stained glass, goldsmiths' and silversmiths' work and jewellery, but also consult rich collections of Old Master prints and drawings, wallpapers, posters, theatrical designs, fashion plates, photographs, illustrations, caricatures, engraved ornament – in short, examples of every type of graphic medium and every period of Western European art.

This huge collection may usefully be likened to the seven eighths of an iceberg which floats beneath the surface of the sea, and much of it is not known to the general public, although individual works can easily be seen on application. But for most visitors their impression of the museum is derived from what they see displayed on the walls, chiefly, though not entirely, oil-paintings.

The Museum's collection of British oil-paintings dates back to the Sheepshank Gift of 1857, consisting of over 200 oil-paintings and nearly 300 watercolours by contemporary painters given with the idea of founding a National Gallery of British Art. They were housed in custom-built galleries and visited by immense crowds, often as many as 3,000 people going through the Galleries in three hours on Monday evenings when the rooms were lit by gas. This gift led to other major donations of British art, notably the presentation in 1888 by his children of paintings, sketches and watercolours by John Constable, which enable us to see every aspect of the great landscape artist's work from his analytical studies of nature to the grandeur of his depiction of Stonehenge silhouetted against a stormy sky broken by a double rainbow.

With the foundation of the Tate Gallery the Victoria and Albert Museum ceased to collect original oils of the British school. It concentrated instead on consolidating the national collections of two specially British art forms – the watercolour and the miniature. The miniature collection includes such powerful portraits as Hans Holbein's *Mrs Pemberton* and Nicholas Hilliard's *Young man with roses*, the visual personification of the hero of a Shakespearean sonnet sequence. The watercolour medium is extremely light sensitive and therefore the collection of over 5,000 works representing more than 1,500 artists is housed in the Print Room, although a changing display is always on view.

Although there has never been a systematic policy of acquiring foreign paintings, several other schools of painting besides the British are strongly represented, largely thanks to the highly personal tastes of the collectors who gave or bequeathed their much loved collections to the museum. A few collectors must be singled out, namely John Jones, a military tailor with an eye for Rococo art who left some fine French eighteenth-century paintings; the Rev. C. H. Townshend whose bequest in 1869 gave the museum a large collection of Swiss mid-19th century paintings, and Constantine Alexamader Ionides, an Anglo-Greek merchant of moderate means but great artistic flair who acquired a splendid collection of French works of all dates ranging from Louis Le Nain to Delacroix, Ingres, Courbet and Daumier, and a splendid group of Barbizon school works, and the first painting by Degas to enter a British collection. From the earliest years of the Museum's history shrewd curators scoured the Continent for works of decorative art, including Gothic banners, fine Florentine and Sienese marriage coffers and painted ceremonial trays. Such works were quite different from the easel pictures acquired at the same time by the National Gallery. Yet students of Italian painting will find much to interest them, with examples of the work of such notable artists from the fourteenth to eighteenth centuries as Botticelli, Carlo Crivelli, Tintoretto, Domenico Beccafumi, Giandomenico Tiepolo and Francesco Guardi. Detached frescos include fine examples by Perino del Vaga and Lodovico Carraçci.

Towering over all other examples of both fine and decorative paintings are the seven Raphael cartoons for tapestry, on loan from the Royal Collection since 1864, amongst the most important of all examples of High Renaissance art. Mainly illustrating scenes from the life of Sts Peter and Paul, they are part of a set commissioned by Pope Leo X in 1515 for tapestries designed for the Sistine Chapel in the Vatican.

English (Canterbury?)
Mid-12th Century
Leaf from a Psalter, possibly the
Eadwine Psalter of 1147
Watercolour and bodycolour on
vellum 38 × 26.7 cm
Inv.no.816-1894

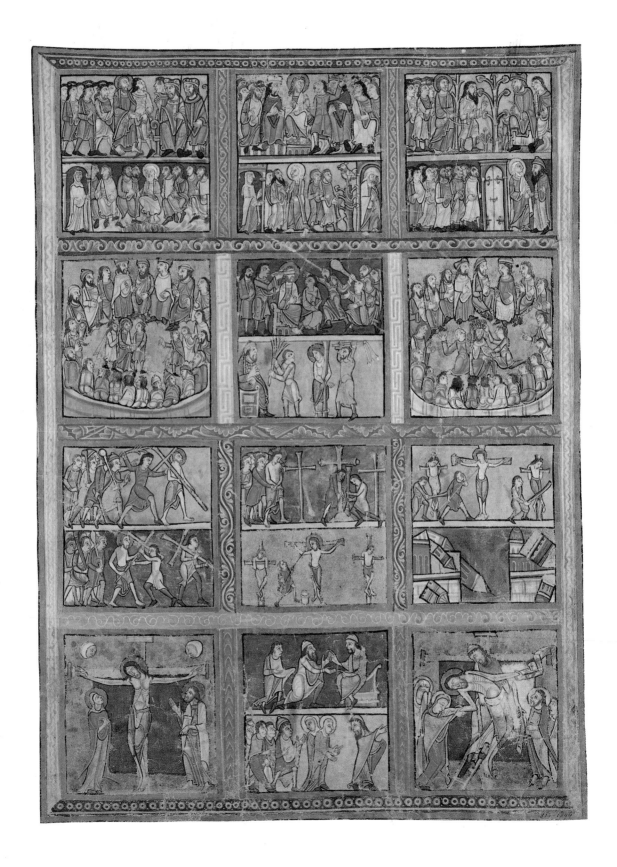

1

French, c1520
Saints
Stained glass, 52.1 × 49.5 cm
Inv.no.c1362-1924
On the left a saints probably St
Stephen or St Lawrence, preaches a
sermon while on the right is
represented a ceremony of ordination.
The style recalls that of the windows
of St-Germain-des-Prés in Paris.

2

**Apollonio di Giovanni (1415-1465)
Italian (Florence)**
Ceremonial *desco da parto: the Triumph
of Love, c1450*
Painted wood, diameter 59.7 cm
Inv.no.144-1869
A *desco da parto* was a ceremonial tray
used in Florence to take food or
sweet-meats to expectant women.
They were often decorated with
mythologies or with allegorical
narratives like this, taken from
Petrarch's poem *I Trionfi.*

1

2

3

4

5

3
Sandro Botticelli (1445-1510)
Italian (Florence)
Smeralda Bandinelli, c1471
Tempera on panel, 65.1 × 40.9 cm
Inv.no.CAI100; Ionides collection
The painting once belonged to Dante
Gabriel Rossetti who communicated
an enthusiasm for Botticelli to other
Pre-Raphaelite artists, notably Edward
Burne-Jones.

4
Bernardo Buontalenti (1536-1608)
Italian (Florence)
Design for an *intermezzo*, *L'Armonia
delle Sfere*, c1589
Ink and watercolour, 38.1 × 55.8 cm
Inv.no.E1186-1931
A Mannerist artist and disciple of
Michelangelo, Buontalenti was by
turns an architect, soldier, painter and
sculptor. He worked chiefly for the
Medici family, producing for them
theatrical designs for *intermezzi* and
firework displays. *Intermezzi* were
divertissements which brought to life
symbolic and allegorical figures. In
this sketch, a design for costume and
decor, *Neccessity* enters through a
break in the clouds holding in her
hand an axe, which joins the two
poles of the universe. This *intermezzo*
was presented at Florence in 1589, on
the occasion of the marriage of
Ferdinand I Duke of Tuscany to the
niece of Catherine de Medicis.

5
Franco di Giovanni de'Russi
Italian (Ferrara or Urbino)
Letter B from an illuminated manuscript,
c1460-80
Painted vellum, 7 × 6.3 cm
Inv.no. E1275-1991
This is one of only two signed works
by this accomplished illuminator, an
anchor in the swirling sea of
attributions made on the basis of
style. The Museum's collection of
illuminated manuscripts is
outstanding.

Raphael (1483-1520)
Italian

The Miraculous Draught of Fishes
Gouache on paper laid on canvas,
319 × 399 cm
On loan from the collection of Her
Majesty the Queen
The series of seven designs for

tapestries by Raphael in the Museum
depict scenes from the lives of St Peter
and St Paul. The tapestries were
intended to hang in the Sistine Chapel
on feast days and were commissioned
by Pope Leo X in 1515. The scene
depicted is an episode from St Luke
(V. 1–10) where Christ miraculously

helps the fishermen fill their nets, and
intimates to St Peter that he will soon
be catching men instead of fish, an
allusion to the rôle of the papacy. The
cranes (symbols of vigilance) were
probably the work of Raphael's
assistant Giovanni da Udine
(1487-1564).

1

Nicholas Hilliard
English 1547?-1619
Young man among Roses, c1587
Watercolour and bodycolour on
vellum 13.4 × 7.3 cm
Inv.no.P163-1910
This portrait, probably of Robert
Devereaux, 2nd Earl of Essex, is one
of the most potent visual images of
the age of Shakespeare.

2

Hans Holbein (1497?-1543)
English
Miniature portrait of Margaret
Pemberton, c1536
Diameter 5.2 cm
Inv.no.P40-1935
The sitter can be identified by the coat
of arms of her husband Robert Pemberton, which is painted on vellum on
the back. Barely a dozen miniatures
are now accepted as being by Holbein
and it is generally agreed that this is
the finest.

3

Nicholas Hilliard (1547?-1619)
English
Queen Elizabeth I, c1588
Body colour on vellum, 4.4 × 3.7 cm
Inv.no.P23-1975

4

Simon Bennick (1483?-1561)
Flemish (Brussels)
The month of April
From a Book of Hours, watercolour on
parchment, 9.5 × 15 cm
Inv.no.E4575-1910
Simon Bennick was a member of an
eminent family of Flemish illustrators.
This is a page of a Calendar, such as
were placed at the beginning of Books
of Hours and indicated the days of
religious festivals. Such illustrations,
fascinating evocations of the life of
the country and court, are often
precise records of specific places. This
scene shows lovers walking and
playing music in a very realistic
setting with microscopically exact
flora and fauna.

5

French, c1500
Louis XII triptych
Painted enamels on copper with
gilding, height 25 cm, width 41.5 cm
Inv.no.552–1877

6

Albrecht Dürer (1471-1528)
German (Nuremberg)
Melancholia I, 1514
Engraving, 23.8 × 18.9 cm
Inv.no.E596-1890

5

6

1
Louis Le Nain (1593-1648)
French
*Landscape with figures ('La Halte du
Cavalier'), c1641*
Oil on canvas, 54.6 × 67.3 cm
Inv.no.CA1208; Ionides collection

2
Mulhouse Album, c1800
Watercolour design for printed cotton
Inv.no.E182-192-1986
A characteristic sheet from an impor-
tant compendium of late 18th to mid-
19th century French. German and
Swiss textile designs.

3
**Arnold Lulls (active late 16th and
early 17th centuries)**
English
Jewellery design
Pencil, wash, body colour and gold
Inv.no.D6-1896

1

2

3

4
François Boucher (1703-70)
French
Madame de Pompadour, 1758
Oil on canvas, 52.4 × 57.7 cm
Inv.no.487-1882; Jones collection
Jeanne Antoinette Poisson (1721-64)
became in 1745 the mistress of Louis
XV receiving the title of Marquise de
Pompadour. Witty and talented, she
became a great patron of learning and
the arts, indicated by Boucher in the
pile of books on which she rests her
elbow, and the open book in her hand.
Boucher excelled in depicting the
richness of fabrics and flowers and is
seen at his best in his portraits of
Madame de Pompadour.

5
Thomas Rowlandson (1756-1827)
English
Vauxhall Gardens
Pen, ink, watercolour, 48.2 × 78.4 cm
Inv.no.P13-1967; purchased with the
assistance of the National Art
Collections Fund
The focal point of the group of
visitors under the trees on the right of
this lively view of the famous London
pleasure garden is the Prince of Wales
(later George IV) whispering to his
lover, the actress Mrs 'Perdita'
Robinson.

4

5

1

William Blake (1757-1827)
English
Satan arousing the rebel angels, 1808
Pen and watercolour, 51.4 × 39 cm
Inv.no.FA697
This is one of 12 illustrations inspired
by Milton's *Paradise Lost.*

1

2

Samuel Palmer (1805-81)
English
In a Shoreham garden, c1829
Gouache, 28.2 × 22.3 cm
Inv.no.P32-1926

This lyrical painting was painted
during the seven years (1826-1833) in
which the artist, a disciple of William
Blake, lived in the idyllic Kent village
of Shoreham, and there produced his
most inspired and mystical work.

3

4

3
John Constable (1776-1837)
English
Study of cirrus clouds, c1822
Watercolour, 11.4 × 17.8 cm
Inv.no.784-1888

4
John Constable (1776-1837)
English
Stonehenge, 1836
Watercolour, 38.7 × 59.1 cm
Inv.no.1629-1888

41

1

1
**Joseph Mallord William Turner
(1775-1851)**
English
*East Cowes Castle, the seat of John Nash
Esq.: the regatta starting on their
moorings, 1828*
Oil on canvas, 91.4 × 128.3 cm
Inv.no.FA210
This work was painted for Turner's
friend the architect John Nash.

2
John Frederick Lewis (1805-76)
English
A halt in the desert, 1855
Watercolour, 36.8 × 49.8 cm
Inv.no.FA532

2

3

3
Honoré Daumier (1808-79)
French
The acrobats ('Les Saltimbanques')
Watercolour, 33.4 × 39.3 cm
Inv.no.CAI120; Ionides collection

4
Jean François Millet (1814-75)
French
Woodsawyers, c1850-52
Oil on canvas, 57 × 81 cm
Inv.no.CAI47; Ionides collection

4

1
Alfred Waterhouse (1830-1905)
English
Design for Manchester Town Hall,
c1868
Watercolour, 78.7 × 63.5 cm
Inv.no.D1882-1908

2
Owen Jones (1809-74)
English
Design for an exhibition building,
c1860
Watercolour, 37.5 × 72 cm
Inv.no.D946-1886

1

2

44

3
Mary Ellen Best (1809-91)
English
Clifton kitchen, 1834
Watercolour, 25.4 × 35.5 cm
Inv.no.P11-1983

4
Charles Frederick Annesley Voysey
(1857-1941)
English
Design for Broadleys, Cartmel,
Lancashire
Watercolour, 73.7 × 52 cm
Inv.no.E252-1913

3

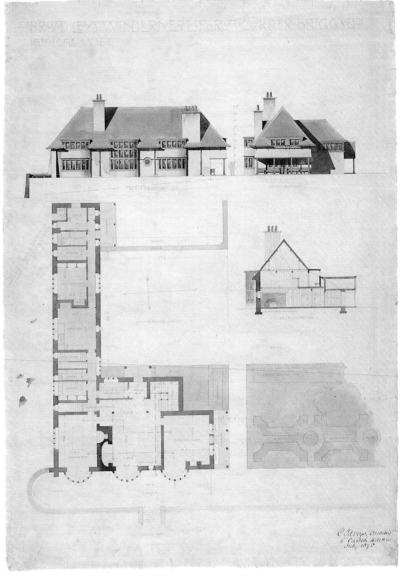

4

1

2

3

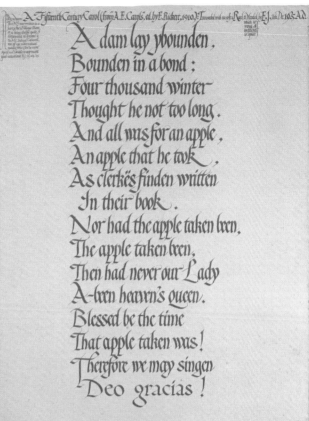

4

5

4
Henri de Toulouse-Lautrec
(1864–1901)
French
Eldorado: Aristide Bruant dans son cabaret, 1892
Coloured lithograph, 139.9 × 96 cm
Inv.no.CIRC564-1974

5
Edward Johnson
English 1872–1944
Calligraphy the 15th century carol
Adam lay ybounden penned in 1925
Pen and ink 56 × 46 cm
Inv.no.L4398-1959

6
Natalia Gontcharova (1881–1962)
Russian
Design for scene II in *L'Oiseau de Feu*, 1926
Pen, watercolour and gold, 60.5 × 66.2 cm
Inv.no.2137-1932
The Museum possesses an impressive collection of designs for the Diaghilev ballets. This is one of the finest for a backcloth, in the revival of *The Fire Bird* at the Lyceum Theatre, London, in November 1926.

6

1
John Hassall (1868-1948)
British
Skegness is SO Bracing, 1903
Colour lithograph, 100.8 × 63 cm
Inv.no.E1326-1931
This was a poster advertising the
London and North Eastern Railway.

2
E. McKnight Kauffer (1890-1954)
American, working in England
*Soaring to Success! Daily Herald – the
Early Bird*
Colour lithograph, 299.7 × 152.2 cm
Inv.no.E35-1973
This poster advertised the relaunch of
the Labour Party's newspaper, the
Daily Herald, on 31 March 1919.

3
Henry C. Beck (1901-74)
British
Original sketch for the first
diagramatic map of London's
underground railways, 1931
Watercolour, 19.1 × 24.4 cm
Inv.no.E814-1979

4
Raymond McGrath (1903-77)
British
Design for Fisher's Restaurant, 1932
Watercolour, 22.7 × 35 cm
Inv.no.CIRC564-1974

1

2

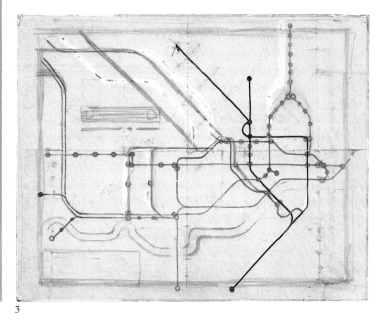

3

4

1

2

3
Henry Moore (1898-1986)
British
Study, from the *Prometheus* series, 1958
Pencil, wax chalk, gouache and Indian ink, 28.9 × 23 cm
Inv.no.CIRC259-1964

4
Robert Rauschenberg (born 1925)
American
From a series of nine prints entitled *Hoarfrost Editions: Pull*, 1974
Screen print on cheese-cloth and silk taffeta with paper bag collage, 226 × 122 cm
Inv.no.E51-1975

3

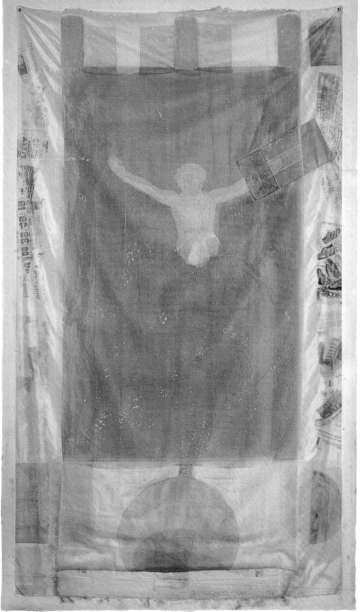

4

1
Paul Nash (1899-1946)
British
The eclipse of the sunflower
Watercolour, 42 × 57.3 cm
Inv.no.P19-1962
Nash wrote of this painting '... a shaft of sunlight breaking through the cloud falls across the form of a giant sunflower bowed by the wind ... the drama of the event, which implies the mystical association of the sunflower and the sun, is heightened by the two opposing eclipses.'

2
Stanley Spencer (1891-1959)
British
Study for *Zacharias and Elizabeth* (Luke I, 5–2), c1913
Pencil and sepia wash, 26.7 × 26.7 cm
Inv.no.P46-1984

Helen Chadwick (born 1953)
British
The oval court, 1986
Mixed media
Inv.no.PLI-222-1987

The oval court was part of Helen Chadwick's exhibition at the Institute of Contemporary Art in 1986 called *Of Mutability*. She used a photocopying machine to reproduce her nude body and various attributes – fish, flesh, fowl, flora, feathers, fruits. The extremely limited possibilities of the machine yielded images both frankly realistic and mysterious. The machine could only take images of a certain size, and so fragments were collaged together producing, as Marina Warner wrote in the catalogue of the exhibition, 'a dreamscape … where existence is no longer actual but only remembered'.

The Furniture and Woodwork Collection

The intended scope of the Furniture and Woodwork Collection, like that of the other collections, was clearly defined by Henry Cole, the Museum's first Director. He wrote in 1863: 'The decorative art of all periods and all countries should be completely represented. Classic art ought not to be omitted, but inasmuch as the British Museum is particularly devoted to the illustration of classic art, it should be represented only to a limited extent.' By Classic art Cole meant ancient Greek and Roman artefacts, an area of collecting which, along with ancient Egypt and Ethnography, is still left to the British Museum. The Victoria & Albert Museum now has a Far Eastern section and an Indian section which cover furniture from those geographical areas.

Thus the Furniture and Woodwork Collection now ranges from the Middle Ages to the present day and embraces the whole of Europe, the Middle East and America. Unlike the other collections such as Ceramics and Metalwork there are no comprehensive Furniture Study Galleries, the exception being the Twentieth Century Study Collection in Galleries 103-106. Thus the furniture and woodwork is displayed along with the other applied arts of similar date in the sequence of the Art and Design Galleries.

Not everything is on display at any one time, but as new galleries are created and old ones re-organized some objects are removed from display whilst others are displayed once again. Those pieces of furniture and examples of woodwork not on display are not necessarily, however, in store; more than 1,000 are on loan and on display in other museums and houses open to the public.

To take Britain first, there are few complete pieces of domestic furniture extant which date from before 1600 – only some chests made for household use, one or two beds and a number of tables and chairs. The Museum has several pieces on display, of which the most celebrated is the Great Bed of Ware, but the best surviving woodwork of this early period is still *in situ* in our churches and cathedrals. The seventeenth- and eighteenth-century furniture collection is the most comprehensive on display in any museum in the world and includes pieces, for instance, designed by Robert Adam, William Kent and William Chambers, but even so it is not as strong as other areas of the Collection. The reason is simple: we are fortunate in this country that many of the most important pieces still furnish the houses for which they were designed.

The nineteenth-century furniture collection includes many of the key pieces of furniture designed and made in Britain at that time. Starting with the 1851 Exhibition and continuing until the late nineteenth century, the Museum perceptively purchased the most remarkable examples of design and craftsmanship exhibited in the International Exhibitions throughout Europe.

These objects make both our British and Continental nineteenth-century collections the strongest and most representative that exist in all fields, including furniture. Since the early 1950s a number of previously under-rated nineteenth-century pieces have been acquired to supplement the original collection.

A wide selection of our comprehensive holdings of twentieth-century British furniture dating from before 1960 is on display in Room 74. That from 1960 to 1991 is displayed as part of the Twentieth-Century Study Collection in Rooms 103-106.

Much more early Continental furniture survives than is the case with Britain, therefore the collection in that field is far stronger. Thus a number of splendid sixteenth-century Italian pieces are on display, including carved chests, chairs and the remarkable lantern in Room 21. Several of these, including the lantern, were acquired by the Museum in the later 1850s as part of the Soulages collection of Renaissance applied art. The later continental furniture of the seventeenth and eighteenth centuries is on display in Rooms 1-7. Whilst the French pieces rarely compete in quality with those in the Royal Collection or The Wallace Collection, the German, Dutch and Italian pieces are of a quality not represented elsewhere in England.

The nineteenth-century Continental and American furniture in Rooms 8 & 9 is again of the highest quality, and was largely purchased new by the Museum. For instance the remarkable collection of Art Nouveau objects – including furniture – in Room 9 was purchased from the Paris Exhibition of 1900.

All the twentieth-century Continental and American furniture on display is in the Study Collection. This includes major pieces by such designers as Le Corbusier, Koloman Moser and Eileen Gray, and the best group of Frank Lloyd Wright pieces outside America. The Museum is actively acquiring contemporary furniture and such pieces are usually put on display in these galleries immediately.

Also included in the Furniture and Woodwork Collection are musical instruments, which constitute a collection of international importance. Most types of Western instruments are represented, but it should be stressed that they were collected for their decoration and ornament as part of the furniture collection and not from a musicological point of view. Indeed whilst most are shown together in Room 40A some, such as Queen Elizabeth's virginals, are displayed with furniture of like period.

1
English, c1525
Table desk
Painted and gilded wood, height
25 cm, width 41 cm, depth 29 cm
Inv.no.W29-1932
This painted and gilded desk bears the
royal arms and the heraldic devices of
Henry VIII and Katherine of Aragon.
It is a unique survival from the rich
and elaborate furniture known to have
been made for the Tudor court. The
figures of Mars, Venus and Cupid are
taken directly from woodcuts by Hans
Burkmair.

2
South German, c1600
Writing desk
Walnut inlaid with bone, height
15 cm, width 48 cm, depth 38 cm
Inv.no.W1-1958
Inlay of this character combining
Mannerist and Grotesque motifs was
made throughout Europe in the later
16th century, but in quality and
technique that on this desk is probably
German. The medallions on the top
are copied from engravings by
Etienne Delaune (1519-83) and inside
the desk are the arms of Francesco
Maria II Duke of Urbino.

3
Italian (Rome), c1560
Chest
Walnut, height 64 cm, width 152 cm
Inv.no.4414-1857
More domestic chests survive in Italy
than in England; they are sometimes
completely painted and gilded. This is
the most splendidly carved example in
the Museum, but painted chests are
also on display. It survives in excellent
condition thanks largely to the fact
that it was acquired in 1857.

4
Italian (Milan), c1550
Mirror
Damascened steel, height 117 cm
Inv.no.7648-1861
This piece represents what was a
relatively common form of domestic
furniture and most would have
been made of carved wood. Few
wooden examples have survived
for although far fewer of the more
expensive high quality metal ones
were made they are of course far less
prone to decay. In the 16th century
Milan was famous for metalworking,
the damascened steel pieces being
particularly prized.

1

2

5
Italian, 1520s
Marquetry of various woods, height
110 cm, width 77 cm
Inv.no.150-1878

This intarsia panel would have formed
part of a whole room decorated in this
way. There would have been a series
of cupboards in the walls concealed
by panels such as this, which appeared
to represent the interiors of the
cupboards themselves.

3

4

5

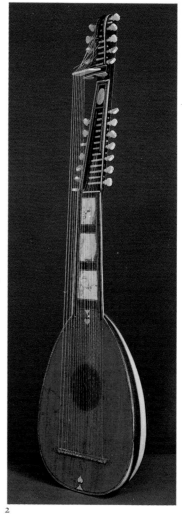

3

1

Hamburg, 1726
Bass Viol
Marquetry of various materials, length
121 cm
Inv.no.1298-1871
An ink label reads *'Martin Voigt in
Hamburg me fecit 1726'*. Voigt is thought
to have been a pupil of the celebrated
Hamburg musical instrument maker
Joachim Tielke.

2

Venetian, 1650s
Theorbo
Marquetry of various materials, length
106 cm
Inv.no.7756-1862
Engraved on the neck *'Christofolo
Choc/Al Aquila Doro/ in Venetia'*. The
back of the neck has marquetry of
snake wood and ivory consisting of
floral scrolls, a bird and a double-
headed eagle.

3

French, 1640
Mandore
Carved pearwood with ebony veneer,
length 42 cm
Inv.no.219-1886
Inscribed in ink 'Boissart 1640'. The
back is carved with the Judgement of
Paris and the head of Medusa.

4

English, *c*1580
The Great Bed of Ware
Carved and painted oak, height
266 cm, width 326 cm
Inv.no.w47-1931
This is the most celebrated piece of
English furniture and since it was
mentioned in one of Shakespeare's
plays it has been described and
depicted many times. As it was made
as a tourist attraction for the White
Hart Inn it was seen by far more
people than if it had been in a normal
house. Ware was a favourite stopping
place on the journey to and from
London and it is quite possible that
Shakespeare actually saw it or indeed
slept in it at the White Hart.

5

German (Augsburg), *c*1600
Cabinet
Ebony with silver mounts, height
38 cm, width 37 cm
Inv.no.M511-1956
Augsburg was particularly famous
throughout the late Middle Ages and
the Renaissance for its goldsmiths and
silversmiths though its furniture
makers were also very active. This
cabinet combines the skills of both
crafts and is a good example of a
group of similar pieces which were
manufactured in the early 17th
century, often for export.

4

5

1

1
Italian (Roman) *c1700*
Table
Carved and gilded wood, marble top,
width 178 cm
Inv.no.w35-1977
This table very clearly demonstrates
the vigour of the Italian Barqoue
carvers who, of course, also applied
their skills to every aspect of interior
decoration and architecture. Sadly it is
not known for which interior this
table was created.

2
French *c1628*
Cabinet
Ebony with gilt metal mounts, height
214 cm, width 156 cm, depth 51 cm
Inv.no.w64-1977
This cabinet is one of the finest pieces
of French early 17th-century furniture
and has traditionally been associated
with Maria de Medici who was
Queen of France until the death of her
husband Henry IV in 1610. It is
certainly of a suitable quality to have
been a royal piece and is similar to
other pieces known to have been
designed for her. The superb mounts
are decorated with figures of Juno,
Jupiter and Minerva and with scenes
from Tasso's *Gerusalemme Liberata*.

2

3
William Kent 1685-1748
English
Pier table, c.1730
Gilded wood, height 89 cm, width
70 cm, depth 46 cm
Inv.no.W14-1971
It seems likely that this table was
designed by Kent for Lord
Burlington's Chiswick House.

4
Grinling Gibbons (1648-1721)
English
Cravat
Carved limewood, height 24 cm,
width 21 cm
Inv.no.W181-1928
When the limewood was new and
white this cravat would have looked

even more like the starched linen
cravat that it was intended to
resemble. It has long been recognized
as perhaps the best example of the
virtuoso carving of England's most
celebrated wood carver. In the 18th
century this piece was in the
collection of Horace Walpole at
Strawberry Hill.

3

5

4

5
**English, late 17th or early 18th
century**
Wallpaper
Height 195 cm, width 60 cm
Inv.no.E5311-1958
This detail of a strip of wallpaper
made up from six separate pieces
came from Orde House, Berwick-on-
Tweed, Northumberland. It is printed

from wood blocks and colour stencils
and has been varnished. The parakeets
and Chinoiserie figures are evidence of
the popularity of Oriental subjects at
this time brought about as a result of
the importation of Chinese and other
goods by the Dutch East India Companies.

1

2

3

1
Dutch c1690
Cabinet
Marquetry of various woods, width
170 cm, height 206 cm, depth 56 cm
Inv.no.w5-1986
Cabinets of this form decorated with
floral marquetry were made in
considerable numbers in Holland in
the late 17th century. The quality of
the marquetry, however, varies
greatly and often becomes very faded.
Here much of the colour remains and
the quality is very high indeed. It can
probably be attributed to Jan van
Mekeren (c1658-1733).

4

2
Mathias Lock (1724-70)
English
Arm-chair, *c1760*
Height 110 cm, width 66 cm, depth
64 cm
Inv.no.w1-1973

3
Bernard Van Riesenberg
(died 1766) French
Commode, 1760
Lacquer, ormolu mounts and marble
slab, height 87 cm
Inv.no.1094-1882
This piece demonstrates the ability of
the best Parisian cabinet-makers to
shape elaborate lacquer panels and
combine them with high quality
ormolu mounts to create Rococo
furniture of great sophistication.

4
Richard Bentley (1708-82)
English
Chair, 1755
Ebonised beech, height 125 cm, width
61 cm, depth 61 cm
Inv.no.w29-1979
Horace Walpole a learned
Mediaevalist was himself partly
responsible for the design of this chair
which set new standards for other
Gothic Revival designers to follow.
The set of dining chairs made by
William Hallett of which this is one
stood in the Great Parlour at
Strawberry Hill.

5
German, *c1750*
Bureau of Augustus III of Saxony
Marquetry of various materials of
ormolu mounts, height 274 cm, width
127 cm
Inv.no.w63-1977
Though the designer and maker of
this bureau have yet to be established
it was almost certainly made in
Dresden and is one of the finest pieces
to survive from the court of Saxony.
The complex marquetry of wood,
metal and other materials and the
elaborate ormolu mounts are of a
quality equal to that achieved by any
of the leading cabinet-makers in Paris
at this date.

6
J. F. Oeben (*c1721-63*)
French
Writing table, *c1755*
Marquetry of various woods with
ormolu mounts, height 69 cm
Inv.no.1095-1882

5

6

The cabinet of Madame de Sérilly
French, 1778
Inv.no.1736-1869
This elegant, yet advanced,
Neoclassical interior was probably
designed by the architect C. N.
Ledoux (1736-1806) for the Hotel de

Sérilly at 106 rue Vieille du Temple It
was created for Madame de Sérilly
(1763-99) who was a great beauty
and of whom there is a bust by
Houdon in The Wallace Collection.
This was the first period room ever to
be acquired by the Museum.

1

2

David Roentgen (1743-1807)
German

Commode, *c.*1780

Marquetry of various woods, ormolu
mounts and a marble top, height
89 cm, width 135 cm, depth 68 cm
Inv.no.w51-1948

The chaste Neoclassical character of
this piece combined with the
marquetry and craftsmanship of the
highest quality is typical of
Roentgen's work. The mechanism
within this piece which at the turn of
the key activates doors and drawers
was also a speciality of his workshop.

3

Robert Adam (1728-92)
British

The Kimbolton Cabinet, 1771

Marquetry of various woods, ormolu
mounts and inlaid marble, height
187 cm, width 178 cm
Inv.no.w43-1949

This cabinet was commissioned
specifically by the Duchess of
Manchester in 1771 to display the fine
Florentine inlaid marble panels dating
from 1709. It is one of Adam's most
rigorously Neoclassical pieces, the
particularly fine mounts were
manufactured especially for this piece
by Matthew Boulton and the whole
made by Ince and Mayhew.

2

3

1
English, c1800
Pier table
Carved and gilt wood with marble
slab, height 91 cm, width 183 cm,
depth 48 cm
Inv.no.W19-1976
This table formed part of the
furnishings designed by Thomas
Hope (1769-1831) for his own house
in Duchess Street, London. Hope was
a well-known connoisseur and
collector who not only designed and
oversaw the creation of a series of
interiors for his own house, but also
published illustrations.

2
Jacob Freres
French, c1800
Cabinet
Amboyna with ormolu mounts and a
marble top, height 119 cm, width
145 cm, depth 51 cm
Inv.no.W9-1971
Made by the firm of Jacob the most
famous firm of Parisian cabinet-makers
of the early 19th-century who worked
extensively for Napoleon. The
designer is not known but may well
have been Charles Percier the
architect.

3
**August Welby Northmore Pugin
(1812-52)**
English
Armoire, 1851
Carved wood with brass mounts,
height 243 cm, width 326 cm, depth
66 cm
Inv.no.25-1852
The Museum purchased this cabinet
directly from the Mediaeval Court of
the International Exhibition of 1851.
It was like a number of pieces in the
Exhibition made to Pugin's designs by
the firm of Crace which was also at
that time collaborating with Pugin on
the furnishing of the New Palace of
Westminster.

1

2

3

4
Thomas Hoffmeister and
T. Behrens
German
Throne, 1851
Carved oak, height 206 cm
Inv.no.w10-1967
One of a pair of thrones shown in the
International Exhibition of 1851 and
purchased by Prince Albert who like
Hoffmeister was a native of Coburg.

5
George Edmund Street (1824-81)
English
Table, 1854
Oak, height 66 cm, diameter 98 cm
Inv.no.w88-1975
A number of these plain, solidly
constructed tables were designed by
Street for the students' bedrooms at
Cuddesdon College near Oxford. The
design demonstrates Street's ability to
combine lessons learnt from a study of
actual Mediaeval furniture and the
furniture of Pugin.

4

5

1

William Burges (1827-81)
English
Cabinet, 1858
Painted wood, height 213 cm, width
140 cm, depth 38 cm
Inv.no.CIRC 217-1961
This cabinet was designed by Burges
for H. G. Yatman, one of his earliest
patrons, and borrowed from him to be
displayed in the International
Exhibition of 1862. It represents the
beginning of the new fashion for
furniture painted in the manner of the
Middle Ages which Burges pioneered.

2
William Morris (1834-96)
English
The Green Dining Room, 1866
The recently established firm of
Morris, Marshall, Faulkner & Co were
commissioned by the Museum to
design and decorate this room as a
dining room. As part of a suite of
three refreshment rooms, it was used
for this purpose until 1939. The
painted panels and the stained glass
were designed by Edward Burne
Jones.

3
Edward William Godwin (1833-86)
English
Sideboard, c1876
Ebonized mahogany with silver plated
metalwork, width 259 cm, depth
56 cm
Inv.no.CIRC38-1953
This is Godwin's most well-known
piece, it was inspired by oriental
prototypes and said when designed to
be in the Anglo-Japanese style. This
style was pioneered in the early 1860s
by artists and designers like Edward
Poynter, William Eden Nesfield and
Richard Norman Shaw and here
Godwin is taking their ideas a stage
further.

1

2

3

1
Ernest Gimson (1864-1919)
English
Cabinet on stand, 1902
Parquetry of various woods with
gilded composition panels, height
188 cm, width 199 cm, depth 48 cm
Inv.no.w27-1977
The furniture designed by Gimson
usually conforms to the ideal of the
Arts and Crafts movement in which
he played a prominent part. The stand
of this cabinet however is inspired by
oriental prototypes and combined
with the gilded composition
ornaments inset into the doors make
this an unusually sophisticated
example of Gimson's work.

2

1

3

2
**Charles Francis Annsley Voysey
(1857-1941)**
English
Chair, 1909
Oak, height 140 cm, width 64 cm
Inv.no.CIRC517-1954
Voysey designed a wide range of
buildings, but he paid close attention
to every aspect of their furnishings
some of which went into commercial
production. Fortunately a wide range
of textiles, wall-papers, light fittings,
carpets and furniture to his designs
survive, though few of his buildings
still retain their original contents.

4

3
Louis Majorelle (1859-26)
French
Arm-chair
Stained walnut, height 122 cm, width
61 cm, depth 56 cm
Inv.no.2001-1900

4
Frank Lloyd Wright (1865-1956)
American
Room and contents, 1937
Inv.no.w9-1974
This room was designed by Wright as
the office of Edgar Kaufmann within
the department store which he owned
in Pittsburgh. Kaufmann also at this
time commissioned Wright to build
for him his country house
Fallingwater. Edgar Kaufmann Jr
(1910-89) who had introduced his
father to Wright presented the room
to the Museum along with all the
furniture and other contents including
the carpet.

5
Koloman Moser (1868-1918)
Austro-Hungarian
Desk and chair. 1903
Made by Caspar Hrazdil. Marquetry
of various woods and brass, desk
height 144 cm, width 120 cm, chair
height 67 cm
Inv.nos.w8-1982, w8a-1982
Moser was one of the founder
members of the Wiener Weskstatte in
1903.

5

1

2

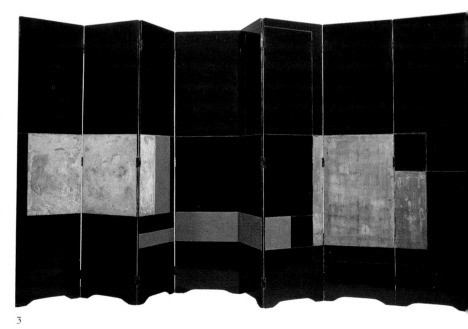

3

1
Vanessa Bell (1879-1961)
British
Screen 1913-14
Painted canvas on wood, height
176 cm, width 208 cm
Inv.no.CIRC165-1964
Vanessa Bell was along with her other
friends from the Bloomsbury Group
deeply influenced by French Post-
Impressionist painting though many
of the works they produced are pale
imitations of their French prototypes.
Here, however, Bell produced a very
fluent painting well designed to act as
a partially folded screen.

2
Gerrit Ritveld (1888-1964)
Dutch
Arm-chair, 1918-20
Stained wood, height 89 cm, width
66 cm, depth 80 cm
Inv.no.W9-1989
This chair is essentially an un-painted
version of the well-known red and
blue chair though it very probably is
of a rather earlier date. The radical
nature of this chair has often been
noted but it may have been inspired
by the plank backed chairs designed
by Frank Lloyd Wright a decade
earlier.

3
Eileen Gray (1917-76)
British
Screen, 1923
Lacquer on wood, height 207 cm
Inv.no.W40-1989
Though Gray was British she spent
most of her life in France and this
screen relates closely to the high
quality lacquer furniture being
produced in Paris in the 1920s by, for
instance, Jean Dunand.

4
Piero Fornasetti (1913-1988)
Italian
Cabinet, 1950
Wood covered with paper, height
223 cm, width 80 cm, depth 40 cm
Inv.no.w21-1983

The overall design of this piece is by
Gio Ponti (1892-1989), Fornasetti
being responsible for the
NeoPalladian applied decoration. The
latter designed a very wide range of
artefacts including ceramics and
textiles many of which were
decorated in this way.

5
John Makepeace (born 1939)
British
Drawers, 1978
Various laminated woods, height
131 cm, width 51 cm
Inv.no.w56-1978

4

5

The Textiles and Dress Collection

The Museum's collection of textiles is one of the largest in the world and spans nearly 5000 years from the third millennium BC to the present day. It illustrates the technical and decorative development of textiles from Europe, the Near and Middle East and Central Asia. The collection of fashionable dress and accessories covers over 400 years extending from the late sixteenth century to the 1990s and concentrates upon European styles which have set, rather than followed, fashion. This overview identifies some highlights of the collection according to technique – woven fabrics, embroidery, printed fabrics, tapestries, lace, carpets and, finally, dress.

The earliest textiles in the Museum are Pharaonic linens excavated from Egyptian tombs; later groups of textiles and garments, also from Egypt, represent late Classical, early Christian and Coptic styles. Archaeological finds and pieces from European churches include silks from late antiquity to the eleventh century from the Byzantine and Islamic Near East. Later Near Eastern and Central Asian woven textiles are also well represented. Italian woven silks show the evolution of design from the thirteenth to the fifteenth centuries. The Italian High Renaissance, is extensively represented by ecclesiastical vestments and fragments of sumptuous woven silks and velvets.

Over 2000 dress and furnishing fabrics reflect expensive tastes in the seventeenth century. Italian luxury textiles dominate but there is a fine selection of silks from France, which marks the next great source of production after 1650. A significant group of eighteenth-century silks woven in Spitalfields and in Lyons document seasonal sylistic changes.

During the momentous industrial expansion of the nineteenth century the Museum made acquisitions from European commercial exhibitions and key pieces came from the Great Exhibition of 1851. British output of the late nineteenth century is well represented. Of particular importance is the collection of William Morris fabrics and the collection of nineteenth-century shawls from Paris, Norwich and Paisley is notable.

Trends in textile design from 1900 to the present are exemplified by furnishing fabrics (woven and printed) from Europe and America. The British collection is unique and unrivalled in its coverage, with work by professional textile designers and leading twentieth-century artists and architects.

The collection of mediaeval emroideries is of international renown. English embroidery known as *opus anglicanum* is epitomised by star pieces including the Clare chasuble and the Syon cope. The post-1500 collection of embroideries has 3000 objects, which range in size and technique from pincushions to table carpets. All western Europe is covered but the English work is of outstanding importance. Panels from the Oxburgh hangings embroidered by Mary Queen of Scots, Bess of Hardwick and their entourage attract much attention.

Lace forms an important part of the collection and ranges from sixteenth-century laces to twentieth-century machine laces.

The famous fifteenth-century Hunting tapestries, which belonged to the Dukes of Devonshire, number among the Museum's masterpieces. The tapestry collection, which incorporates the National collection of English tapestry, also includes notable French and Brussels tapestries of the sixteenth to twentieth centuries. As well known as the Gothic Hunting tapestries is the carpet from the mosque at Ardabil dated 1539-40. The carpet collection (dating from the ninth to the twentieth century) represents work from Iran, Turkey, Turkestan, India, North Africa, America and Europe, with some fine pieces of English Turkeywork.

One of the Museum's most popular attractions is the Dress Collection, which charts the development of male and female fashionable attire and a multiplicity of accessories from the sixteenth century to today. The earliest garment on public display is a rare linen shirt dating from the 1540s. Of exceptional interest is a group of seventeenth-century outfits showing what people of affluence would have worn. The group includes a woman's slashed gown (c1600), men's suits of the 1630s and 1680, several embroidered cloaks, richly decorated jackets and bodices for women and a rare supportasse of satin covered card.

The collection of eighteenth-century formal dresses in luxurious silks is extensive and covers the most fashionable styles of the century. Supported by excessively wide, hooped petticoats, two magnificent court dress (mantuas), of the 1740s, are of special interest. Men's eighteenth-century dress is represented by formal full dress or court suits of elaborately embroidered silks and velvets. The fashion revolution of the 1790s and the subsequent popularity of the classical style and the complexities of changing modes of the nineteenth century with their sometimes alarming underpinnings and diverse dress fabrics and trimmings are well illustrated by the collection.

Although its holdings show aspects of late nineteenth-century and early twentieth-century rational attire, artistic dress, sportswear and highly decorated Edwardian fashions, the collection is not strong in these areas. It received a boost with the purchase of elegant clothes dating from 1905 to 1920 belonging to Miss Heather Firbank, sister of the writer Ronald Firbank. Men's fashions for the twentieth century are well represented by bespoke tailor-made day and evening wear, leisure wear and top designer clothes. Post-1920 the collection was enriched by the gift of garments and accessories representing the work of over 70 top international designers, which was put together by Sir Cecil Beaton. The most recent part of the collection records developments in the world of high fashion from the 1960s to the 1990s.

1

East Mediterranean, 8th or 9th century
'Lion-tamers'
Woven silk, compound twill,
40 × 32 cm
Inv.no.7036-1860

2

English, 1272-94
The Clare chasuble: detail from the back, showing *the Virgin and Child*
Satin embroidered with silver, silver-gilt and silk thread in underside couching, split stitch and laid and couched work, 115.6 × 66 cm
Inv.no.673-1864

3

English, 1300-20
The John of Thanet panel, originally from a cope: *Christ in Majesty*
Silk twill embroidered with silver, silver-gilt and silk thread in underside couching and split stitch, details in pearls, 100 × 41.5 cm
Inv.no.T337-1921

1

2

3

1

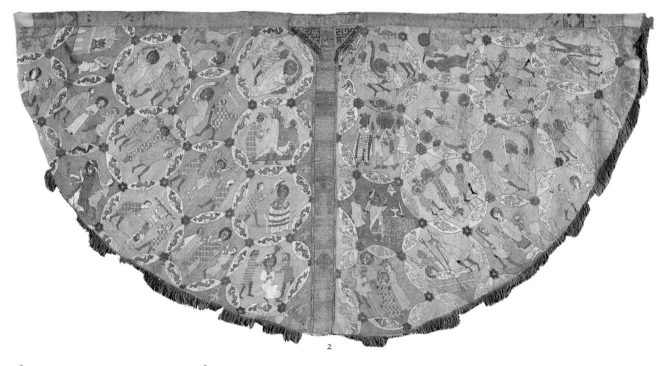

2

1
Spanish, 1530
Altar frontal
Cloth of gold and silver on velvet,
embroidered with gold, silver and silk
thread, in split, brick and satin stitch,
132 × 274 cm
From the Church of San Juan de los
Reyes, Toledo; inv.no.T141-1969

2
German, early 14th century
The Hildesheim cope: *Scenes of the
martyrdom of apostles and saints*
Linen embroidered with gold and silk
thread, in brick stitch and couched
work, 145 × 286 cm
Inv.no.17-1873

3
English, 1330-50
The Butler-Bowdon cope (detail)
Velvet embroidered with silver, silver-
gilt and silk thread in underside and
surface couching, split and satin stitch
and couched work with French knots,
162.8 × 349 cm
Inv.no.T36-1955

4
**Flemish (probably Arras), late
1420s-early 1430s**
The boar and bear hunt
Tapestry, woven in wool,
384 × 1022 cm
Inv.no.T204-1957
The famous 15th-century hunting
tapestries, owned by the Dukes of
Devonshire from the late 16th
century, reflect the interest of the time
in hunting, both as a courtly pastime,
for which elaborate etiquette evolved,
and as a source of fresh meat in
winter. This detail is taken from the
earliest of the four Hunts that now
form a set though originally they
were woven at different times over a
quarter of a century with at least two
up-datings of the costume.

3

4

1
English, late 16th century
The Bradford table carpet (detail)
Linen canvas embroidered with silk
thread in tent stitch, 175.5 × 396 cm
Inv.no.T134-1928
The wide border has scenes of
contemporary life.

2
English, *c*1570
'Elephant' panel from the Oxburgh
hangings
Linen canvas, embroidered with silk
thread in cross stitch, 26.5 × 26.5 cm
Inv.no.T33gg-1955

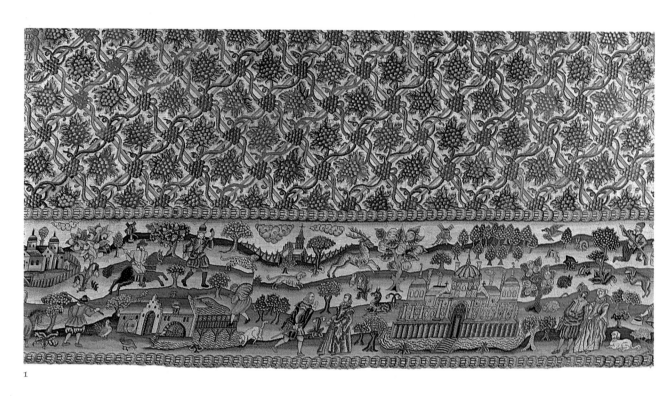

1

2

3

3
Jane Bostocke (active 1598)
English
Sampler, 1598
Linen embroidered with metal and silk thread in a variety of stitches including back, cross, chain, satin, arrowhead and buttonhole stitch,

signed and dated, 42.5 × 35.5 cm
Inv.no.T190-1960

4
English (Sheldon workshop), 1588
Tapestry map of Oxfordshire and Berkshire with areas of surrounding counties (fragment showing Hampton Court and Woking; figures in the border are *Temperance* and *Mercury*)
Tapestry, woven in wool and silk, 126 × 65 cm
Inv.no.T61-1954

4

5

5
English, *c*1630
Doublet, breeches and cloak
Yellow satin, pinked and braided to resemble slashing.
Inv.nos.T58-1910, T58a-1910, T58b-1910
This suit displays the fashionable highwaisted doublet with the extended tabs or skirts that adjust the length to hip level, worn with tapered knee-length breeches known as 'Venetians'. The cloak is circular with a deep collar. The effect of slashing has been achieved by painstaking construction of hundreds of narrow strips of satin each of which has been bound over a stiffened interlining and finished with braided decoration. Finally each in turn has been laid on a piece of satin with pinked edges.

1

2

3

1
Francis Cleyn (active 1640-70)
English (Mortlake or Lambeth)
Circe and Picus (detail), from the
tapestry series known as *The horses*
Tapestry, woven in silk and wool,
with the arms of Henry Mordaunt,
Earl of Peterborough, 376 × 482 cm
Inv.no.T212-1985

2
English, 1744
Court mantua and petticoat
White ribbed silk embroidered to
shape in flowers of natural colours in
long and short stitches and French
knots
Inv.nos.T260-1969, T260a-1960
The term 'mantua' was applied to a
robe with a train which was arranged
behind in a complicated system of
looped cords and folds.

3
Philippe de Lasalle (1723-1803)
French (Lyons), c1770
Woven silk
55.9 × 139.7 cm
Inv.no.T187-1931

4
Charles Le Brun (1619-90)
French (Gobelins)
*Residences Royales: Château de Vincennes,
The Month of July* (detail showing
Louis XIV hunting at Vincennes in
July), late 17th century
Tapestry, woven in wool and silk,
334 × 345 cm
Inv.no.T371-1977

4

1

1

English, 1815-22
Nightgown and 'Cossack' trousers
The nightgown of cream flannel
imitating ermine; the trousers of
unbleached linen
Inv.nos.CIRC718/7-1912, T213-1962
The double-breasted nightgown is
influenced by military uniform. The
'Cossack' trousers became fashionable
after the Tsar made a state visit to
London in 1814.

2

3

4

5

1

2

3

1
English, 1905
Travelling gown
Woollen face cloth trimmed with
braid, velvet, chemical lace and net
Inv.no.T421-H-1977

2
Paul Poiret
French (Paris), 1912
'Sorbet' evening ensemble (skirt and
tunic)
Satin and chiffon with bead
embroidery and fur trim
Inv.nos.T385-1976, T385a-1976

3
Alexander Calder (1898–1976)
American
Tapestry: *Autumn leaves*, 1971
Wool on cotton warp, woven by
Pinton Frères, Aubusson,
165 × 237 cm
Inv.no.T503-1974

4
Christian Dior
French (Paris)
'Bar' suit, Spring/Summer 1947
Silk jacket, woollen skirt
Inv.no.T376&A-1960
This was one of the most popular
models in Dior's famous 'New Look'
collection which caused a furore in the
Press and banished the wide
shouldered, short skirted styles worn
by women in wartime Europe.
Returning to the silhouette termed
'feminine', its impact depends upon
soft curves at shoulders and hips, a
miniscule waist and spreading skirts.

5
English (London)
Day outfit – Coat, shirt and skirt, hat,
belt, 1979
Coat, shirt and skirt by Wendy
Dagworthy; hat by Herbert Johnson;
belt by Christopher Trill
Inv.no.T225 to T236-1980

6
Marion Dorn
English
Exotique, 1938
Screen-printed linen, 183 × 127 cm
Inv.no.CIRC.282-1938
Marion Dorn was born in San
Francisco and came to England in the
early 1920s. She was eventually
persuaded to move back to the USA
in 1940 but in the intervening period
she established a reputation here as
one of the leading textile and carpet
designers. This particular printed
cotton entitled 'Exotique' was
designed for Messrs Donald Bros Ltd,
Dundee.

4

5

6

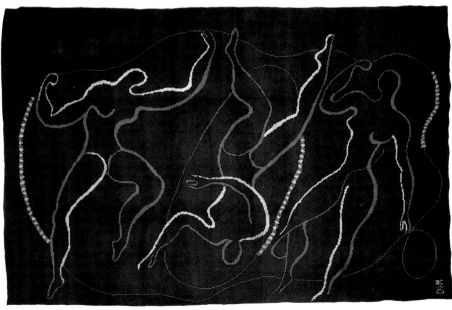

7

7
V. Bobermann for Maison de Décoration Intérieure Moderne French (Paris)
Carpet, 1928-29

Wool pile on jute warp, signed 'DIM',
299.7 × 194.3 cm
Inv.no.T366-1977

The Ceramic and Glass Collections

The ceramic and glass collections were largely formed in the nineteenth century, with the original intention of displaying examples of good design for the improvement of British manufacture, but later with the aim of collecting representative objects of the main cultures – Europe, China, Islam – from the medieval period onwards. Not unnaturally, England takes the largest share, well demonstrating the major part played by Staffordshire in the history of world ceramics with its development of creamware in the eighteenth century: there are good collections of delftware, slipware, Staffordshire pottery, art pottery, and studio pottery which, along with modern industrial wares, are actively collected. The eighteenth-century porcelain benefitted greatly from the gift in 1884 of the important collection of Lady Charlotte Schreiber (kept together in Room 139), which is strong in Chelsea, Bow, Derby and Worcester, as well as in Staffordshire pottery. The eponymous 'Girl-in-a-Swing' and a large group of 'A-Marked' porcelains are amongst the ceramic mysteries awaiting attribution. The nineteenth century is well covered, not only from bequests of grand painted ornamental wares of Worcester and Derby, but also with groups of teawares from many smaller factories made in the nineteenth and twentieth centuries.

The arrangement of the Ceramic Galleries was designed to trace the world-wide development of pottery and porcelain. From one end, token groups of Greek and Roman pottery lead on to the Near East and the earliest use of tin-glaze, to Spain, Italy and Germany. The collections of Italian maiolica are probably the best in the world, while those of Turkish and Persian pottery are outstanding. From the other end of the Galleries, Chinese and Japanese pottery and porcelain lead into the European porcelain, where the history of its discovery and spread can be traced, from Meissen to Vienna, Italy and elsewhere. Masterpieces include the Meissen *Goat*, modelled by Kaendler for the Japanese Palace at Dresden, and an unparalleled collection of Medici porcelain. Because of the disposition of the Galleries, French ceramics are displayed on the floor below, with a comprehensive collection of faience and porcelain in Gallery 128, and the rare Palissy and St Porchaire pottery in 127.

Apart from the Islamic and Spanish collections, all tiles are displayed together, partly in drawers for ease of reference. English painted enamels are included amongst the porcelain, while Limoges enamels are displayed together beside the French ceramics. A representative selection of the important stained glass collection is displayed in various Galleries. Gallery 138 houses a changing display of twentieth century ceramics, alternating with special exhibitions.

The history of glass from Egyptian core-wound, through blown and pressed to art glass and modern sculptural pieces, is contained in Gallery 131, which it is hoped will shortly undergo a major transformation. The Continental engraved glass and the comprehensive series of English drinking glasses, from the earliest Ravenscroft lead-glass onwards, are noteworthy.

Masterpieces are often to be found in the Art and Design Galleries, for example Gallery 4 which is modelled on a *Porzellankammer*, containing outstanding examples of Continental eighteenth-century ceramics, and Galleries 8-9 which contain important and large pieces acquired by the Museum from international exhibitions during the nineteenth century. The Materials and Techniques Galleries also emphasize the history of design, from the hand of the practised but illiterate ancient potter to the drawing board of the modern international architect or designer.

1
Venetian, late 15th century
Goblet
Green glass, enamelled and gilt,
height 17.1 cm
Inv.no.409-1854

2
Italian (Cafaggiolo), early 16th century
A maiolica painter at work
Tin-glazed earthenware (maiolica), diameter 23.5 cm
Inv.no.1717-1855

3
English, early 14th century
Scenes from *The Infancy of Christ*
Tile with *sgraffito* decoration, length 36 cm
From Tring parish church;
inv.no.470-1927

4
Spanish, 'Hispano-Moresque' (Manises), mid-15th century
Drug jar (*albarello*)
Tin-glazed earthenware painted in blue and lustre, height 39.4 cm
Inv.no.52-1907

The later Middle Ages saw great changes in the techniques and use of ceramics and glass. Whereas the English tiles from Tring are drawn directly on to clay by a monk in the manner of manuscript illumination, the tin-glazed pottery of Spain and Italy provided a ground for painting in a limited range of colours, or for decoration in the Near Eastern lustre technique. These highly decorative effects in turn encouraged patronage of potters and glassmakers by wealthy and discerning clients: the Spanish drug jar bears the device of a pharmacy, probably monastic, while the slightly later goblet and dish show respectively the refinement and richness of Venetian enamelling on glass and a rare glimpse into the studio of a maiolica painter, who is closely observed by his prospective customers.

3

1

2

4

1
South German, 1604
Ceremonial beaker and cover
(*Reichsadlerhumpen*)
Glass, painted in enamel colours,
height 49.2 cm
Inv.no.C314 and A-1936

2
**English (London, Pickleherring
factory), 1635**
Charger, painted with *The Fall of Man*
Tin-glazed earthenware (delftware),
diameter 48.3 cm
Inv.no.C26-1931

3
Italian (Florence), late 16th century
Bottle
Soft-paste 'Medici' porcelain, height
17.5 cm
Inv.no.229-1890

4
Netherlandish, 17th century
Wine glass 'façon de Venise'
Clear, red, yellow and *lattimo* glass,
height 23.5 cm
Inv.no.594-1903

1

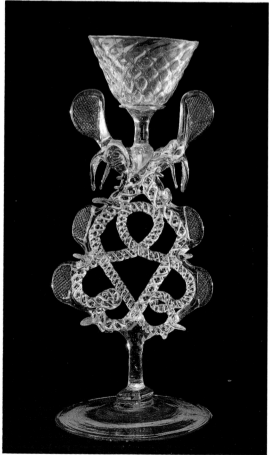

3

2

4

The Ceramic Collections are studded with crucial landmarks in the spread and developments of art and design. 'Medici porcelain', an attempt by the second Grand Duke of Tuscany to copy Chinese porcelain in Florence in the 1570s, is represented, despite its extreme rarity, by no less than nine examples. Similarly, there are several of the rare early experiments by the Venetian glass maker Verzelini to produce clear glass goblets in London in the late 16th century, the beginning of a native industry which, a hundred years later, culminated in George Ravenscroft's lead glass. The delftware charger of 1635 is thought to have been made for the daughter and son-in-law of the Netherlandish potter Christian Wilhelm, who had been largely responsible for establishing the important technique in London, possibly to commemorate the firing of a new kiln at the Pickleherring pottery in Southwark.

6

5

5
English (London, glasshouse of Giacomo Verzelini), 1581
Goblet
Clear glass, diamond-engraved by Anthony de Lisle, height 20.6 cm
Inv.no.c523-1936

6
Dutch, second half 17th century
Drinking glass (*Roemer*)
Diamond-engraved in the style of W. Mooleyser, height 20.4 cm
Inv.no.c293-1936

1

2

3

1
English (Staffordshire), mid-18th century
Pew group
Salt-glazed stoneware, hand modelled,
height 16 cm
Inv.no.c6-1975

2
English (Fulham, factory of John Dwight), 1673
Lydia Dwight
Salt-glazed stoneware, hand modelled,
height 28.6 cm
Inv.no.1054-1871

3
English (Chelsea), *c1755*
Chinese musicians
Porcelain, painted in enamel colours,
height 35.6 cm
Inv.no.c40-1974

4
German (Meissen), *c1770*
Part dinner service
Porcelain, the figures modelled by
J. J. Kaendler
Inv.no.c238- to c256-1921

5
French (Sèvres), *c1780*
Vase with *Jupiter seducing Callisto* after
Boucher
Porcelain, with *bleu nouveau* ground
colour, height 47 cm
Said to have been presented by Louis
XVI to Tippoo Sahib in 1788;
inv.no.747-1882

6
German (Nymphenburg), *c1760*
Columbine, from the Commedia
dell'Arte
Porcelain, modelled by Franz Anton
Bustelli, height 19.7 cm
Inv.no.c82-1954

Following John Dwight's successful
patent for making salt-glazed
stoneware at Fulham in 1671, factories
in Staffordshire during the 18th
century perfected the mass-production
of stoneware upon which their
expansion depended. Later they
turned to moulded figures after some

delightfully naive early attempts at
hand-modelling, typified by the rare
pew groups. The making of porcelain
came late to England, so that the
comparative sophistication of Chelsea
owed much to its Flemish proprietor
and modellers. In contrast, the well-
established factory at Meissen

produced a reliable greyish hard-paste
and employed excellent native
decorators, and modellers such as
J. J. Kaendler, while the French Royal
factory at Sèvres further embellished
its soft-paste with rich ground colours,
lavish painting and gilding.

4

5

6

1
English (Minton)
Food Warmer, described in the
Minton Pattern Book as a 'Ni lamp',
c1820
Bone-china, painted in enamel colours
and gilt, height 22.5 cm
Inv.no.c601 to 601e-1935

2
American (L. C. Tiffany), 1896
Bottle
Iridescent 'favrile' glass, height
40.6 cm
Inv.no.512-1896

3
William Burges
English
Decanter, 1865
Glass, mounted in chased and parcel
gilt silver, set amethysts, opals, other
stones and ancient coins; maker's mark
Richard A Green, height 28 cm
Inv.no.CIRC.857-1956

4
English (Newcastle-upon-Tyne),
c1770
Wine glass
Armorials, including figures of coal
miners, painted by Beilby, height
18.4 cm
Inv.no.c623-1936

5
French (Nancy, Daum Frères), late
19th century
Bottle
Glass, cut, engraved and gilt, height
18.4 cm
Inv.no.C1213-1917

6
French (René Buthaud), c1928-30
Vase
Stoneware, painted in enamel colours,
height 23.5 cm
Inv.no.c292-1987

7
American (Dale Chihuly), 1985
Glass form, 'Davy's gray sea form set
with black lip wraps', width 66 cm
Inv.no.C111- to C111g-1987

8
French (René Lalique), c1925
Lamp
Moulded and etched glass with plastic
base, height 45 cm
Inv.no.c73 to B-1972

1

2

3

4

European glass remained mainly functional until the mid-19th century when decorative pieces began to appear, using a blend of revived earlier styles and techniques. The reaction to this historicism brought art glass, which relied on cameo-cutting, acid-etching and a range of newly discovered surface treatments to produce a variety of textures and colours. The influence of Islamic glass and the lustrous colours of deliberate iridescence can be seen in this Tiffany bottle, while the Lalique lamp combines the contrast of matt and polished, moulded and engraved glass with the practicality of a table-lamp. Dale Chihuly is one of the greatest exponents of studio or 'hot' glass today, making evocative, fragile and elaborate decorative forms.

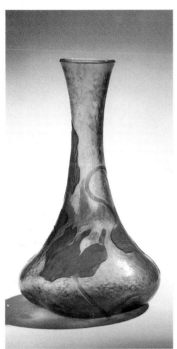

5

6

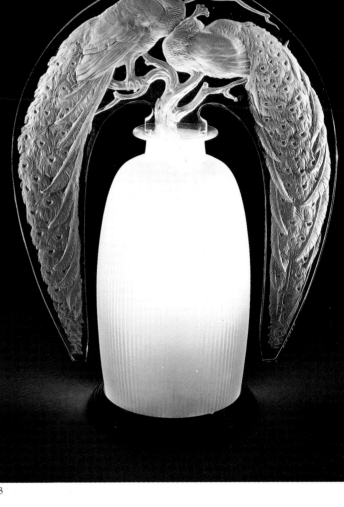

8

7

1

English (factory of William de Morgan), late 19th century
Group of pottery with lustre decoration, maximum height 23.8 cm
Inv.nos.c421-1919, c4-1971, 859-1905, CIRC193-1919

2

English (London, Martin Brothers), 1899
Vase and cover in the form of an owl
Salt-glazed stoneware, height 26 cm
Inv.no.c491 and A-1919

1

2

3

4

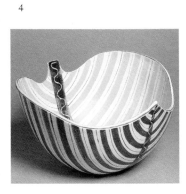

5

3
English (Lucie Rie), c1980
Porcelain bowl, with incised
decoration, width 20.8 cm
Inv.no.c46-1982

4
American (Rudy Autio), 1983
Stoneware sculpture, 'Two ladies
averting the angry swallow', height
55.8 cm
Inv.no.c27-1986

5
**Swedish (designed by Stig
Lindberg, made at Gustavsberg),
1951**
Salad bowl
Earthenware, painted and incised,
length 25 cm
Inv.no.CIRC52-1952

6
**Finnish (designed by Oiva Toikka,
made at Nuutajärvi), 1969**
Glass form, 'Lollipop isle', height
38 cm
Inv.no.CIRC444-1969

7
English (Bernard Leach), c1957
Vase
Stoneware with *tenmoku* glaze, height
34 cm
Inv.no.CIRC115-1958

8
English (Gordon Baldwin), 1984
Stoneware form, 'Avis II No.4', height
58.8 cm
Inv.no.c155-1984

As with art glass, art pottery appeared
towards the end of the 19th century,
offering scope for widely differing
techniques: surface decoration
including lustre, hand modelling and
special glazes. The stylized, chaste
pots designed by William de Morgan
contrast with the wilder stonewares of
the eccentric Martin Brothers: from
these roots grew the English studio
pottery movement, which today has
equally divergent schools, epitomised
by Bernard Leach and Lucie Rie but
including also a strong sculptural
element, which has been still further
developed in America by artists such
as Rudy Autio. Parallel with these
movements, industrial design,
especially Scandinavian, combines
mass-production with original,
functional and attractive form. The
Ceramic Collections include abundant
examples of all these streams of
modern art and design.

6

7

8

Metalwork and Jewellery Collection

The Metalwork Collection in the Victoria and Albert Museum is one of the most diverse and comprehensive in the world, consisting of more than 40,000 mediaeval, Renaissance, Baroque and more recent pieces made of gold, silver, iron, brass, copper, tin, lead and precious stones, as well as twentieth-century alloys and some plastics.

The holdings range in date from 2000 BC to the present, although only items dating from after the ninth century AD are actively collected and the great majority of acquisitions now date from the twentieth century. Their scope is international and includes jewellery and metalwork not only from all parts of Europe but also from the Islamic world (see p.151); recent acquisitions include jewellery by American and Japanese artists. In several areas, for instance cutlery; rings; watches; mortars; ormolu (gilt bronze); mediaeval and nineteenth-century enamels; British biscuit tins – the Metalwork Collections are extensive enough to present a more or less complete picture of the development of design. In objects of certain periods, for instance Romanesque and post-mediaeval copper- and brasswork, the Museum can boast of one or more examples of virtually every kind of object known. Such claims cannot be made for all fields the Collection represents – sometimes because the rate of survival has been extremely low – but the number of individual treasures of outstanding significance or beauty is very high: the following pages can only pick out a few.

The Mediaeval Treasury contains some outstanding and rare pieces of early metalwork made for liturgical use, such as the Gloucester candlestick and the Eltenberg reliquary. English goldsmiths' work of the later Middle Ages includes a censer, in the form of a Gothic tower, with an incense boat, both from Ramsey Abbey, and the Studley bowl, a domestic drinking vessel engraved with an alphabet. Masterworks of Mosan or Mosan influenced enamelling include the richly coloured biblical scenes on the twelfth-century Balfour ciborium.

Particular mention should be made of the English silver, which ranges in date from 1300 to the 1980s. Just as the Sculpture is a National collection, so, too, the Victoria and Albert's holdings of English silver have special status as the National collection of silver. After the Reformation, domestic objects predominate although the development of liturgical plate can be studied in the English Church Plate Gallery (Room 84). The later English Art and Design Galleries are rich in important plate by the leading designers and goldsmiths of the eighteenth, nineteenth and twentieth centuries from Paul de Lamerie and Robert Adam to the masters of the Gothic revival such as A. W. N. Pugin and William Burges. Christopher Dresser, C. R. Ashbee and Harold Stabler bridge the transition to modernism. Magnificent silver centrepieces from the Rococo period (by Nicholas Sprimont, Room 58) and the late nineteenth century (Room 118) are on show, although examples of presentation Regency silver can best be studied in the Wellington Museum, Apsley House, where three important silver dinner services are exhibited.

The collections of European silver, particularly German secular church pieces of the fifteenth to the seventeenth centuries and the Hispanic secular silver, are unusually rich, thanks to the generosity of Dr W. L. Hildburgh. Since French silver rarely survives, the Museum has been fortunate in two major acquisitions, the fourteenth-century Rouen treasure (spoons and bowls) and the Burghley nef, a Renaissance table ornament made in Paris in 1528. Mediaeval Italy is represented by copper-gilt objects and by ecclesiastical plate such as the Bergamo processional cross (c1390). An outstanding example of Baroque goldsmiths' work is the Lomellini ewer and basin, part of a buffet set made for a Genoese merchant prince in 1622 (Room 3). The German silver, the largest collection outside Germany, predominates in the European Silver galleries (Rooms 68-69) where there are smaller displays of Dutch, Flemish, Russian and South American plate.

The art of the blacksmith is another area where the collection is outstanding – some 2000 examples of wrought ironwork, from locks and firebacks to railings and shopsigns, both English made and from Spain, Italy and Germany. The holdings of European pewter are again significant. Other special fields of importance are edged weapons and guns from the Renaissance to the early nineteenth century. The clocks are largely displayed in the Musical Instruments Gallery, although in the English Renaissance galleries (Rooms 52-55) there are the earliest London-made brass clock (1588), a silver tableclock made for James I and Charles I's travelling timepiece.

The Jewellery Gallery exhibits some 5000 objects made in silver, gold and precious stones. Among the earliest are Saxon brooches and Byzantine earrings. Important medieval jewels include an English gold rosary and a group of posy rings; from the Renaissance are portrait miniatures in enamelled goldcases. Jewellery in base metals as well as precious is strongly represented, from early nineteenth-century Prussian iron jewellery to contemporary plastic, feather and ceramic pieces.

The Museum actively collects the work of leading contemporary designers. In the past decade it has commissioned a chandelier from David Watkins, the Carrington Cup from Kevin Coates and the Seal of the Trustees from Malcolm Appleby.

The arts of working metal were highly regarded by the founders of the Museum, who as early as 1853 initiated a programme of electrotype reproductions of exemplary historic pieces both from its own collection and from treasuries and museums from Russia to Spain. This undertaking runs parallel to the formation of the Museum's famous collection of casts from outstanding monuments of sculpture.

1
English, c1104-13
The Gloucester candlestick
Cast gilt copper alloy with niello. An inscription states that it was given by Peter (abbot 1104-13) and his congregation to St Peter's abbey,

Gloucester (now Gloucester cathedral). Decorated with interwoven foliage, men and monsters, with the symbols of the four Evangelists around the central knop. Height 58.4 cm
Inv.no.7649-1861

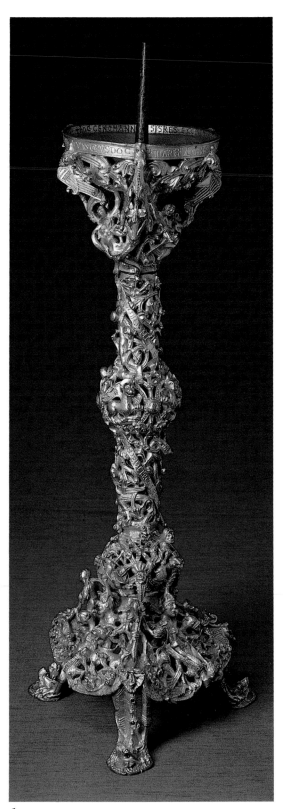

1

2

3

2
English, 1290-96
The Valence casket
Copper alloy engraved and gilt. Decorated with *champlevé* enamel showing the armorial bearings of the Valence family (earls of Pembroke), and other noble and royal families. Height 9.5 cm
Inv.no.4-1865

3
Mosan, c1150-75
One of the Rolls plaques: *Alexander ascending into the sky*
Copper gilt, engraved and enamelled in *champlevé*, 10.2 × 10.2 cm
Inv.no.M53a-1988

Only a fraction of the many metalwork objects produced during the Middle Ages have survived into the 20th century; many have been reworked, melted down or lost. Nevertheless, the Museum's oustanding collection of mediaeval metalwork displays the rich variety of the period.

Many 12th-century pieces such as the Gloucester candlestick and the Rolls plaque are the products of church patronage. The candlestick would have stood upon the altar of a church, whilst the Rolls plaque is one of a number of plaques showing scenes from the Life of Christ and associated subjects, which were originally attached to a larger object such as an altar frontal or shrine.

The Valence casket provides an example of a secular commission; it was probably intended to safeguard jewels or precious trinkets.

1
Rhineland, late 12th century
The Eltenberg reliquary
Alloy of copper gilt, with *champlevé* enamel, walrus and elephant ivory carvings on an oak foundation. Decorated with seated figures of *Christ and the eleven Apostles*, standing figures of the *prophets*, and plaques depicting scenes from the life of Christ: the *Holy Family*, the *Journey of the Magi* (19th-century replacements), the *Crucifixion* and the *Three Maries by the Tomb*. Height 54.6 cm
Inv.no.7650-1861

2
English, *c*1400
The Studley bowl
Silver, parcel gilt. Engraved with the letters of the alphabet in Gothic script. Height 14 cm, diameter 14.6 cm
Inv.no.M1-1914

1

2

3

3
English, *c*1320
The Swinburne pyx
Silver, engraved, parcel gilt, formerly covered with translucent enamel. Decorated with the Lamb of God underneath and the Head of Christ inside. The lid shows the *Virgin and Child* on the outside, and the *Nativity* inside. Diameter 5.7 cm
Inv.no.M15-1950

4

4

Southern German, 1351

The Reichenau crosier

Copper gilt, with plaques of silver and translucent enamel. An inscription states that it was made in 1351 for the Benedictine abbey of Reichenau, whilst Everard von Brandis was non-resident abbot and Nicholas von Guttenberg treasurer. Decorated with plaques showing the *Virgin and Child*, the *Three Magi*, *St Mary Magdalen* and the first abbot *St Firminius*, and figures of the donors and the *Virgin and Child*.

Height 52.1 cm

Inv.no.7950-1862

5

English, *c*1350

The Ramsey Abbey censer

Silver gilt. Modelled on the design for a chapter house. Height 27.4 cm, diameter 13.6 cm

Inv.no.268-1923

5

1
French (Paris), *c*1527-28
The Burghley nef
Nautilus shell mounted in silver,
parcel gilt. Showing figures of *Tristram
and Iseult* playing chess on their
journey from Ireland to Cornwall.
Made by Pierre le Flamand. Height
35.2 cm
Inv.no.M60-1959

2
Italian (Milan), *c*1580
Burgonet
Steel embossed and damascened with
gold and silver. Attributed to the
armourer Lucio Picinino. Height
30.5 cm
Inv.no.M189-1921

3
Italian (Pesaro), *c*1545
Stirrups, from an armour in classical
style
Iron, damascened with gold and silver
vine-leaf decoration. Made for
Emperor Charles V. Attributed to the
goldsmith-armourer Bartolommeo
Campi. Height 20.3 cm
Inv.nos.662-1910, 662a-1910; Salting
bequest

4
English, *c*1600
The Armada jewel
Enamelled gold set with diamonds and
Burmese rubies, enclosing a miniature
painting of Queen Elizabeth I on
vellum stuck to card. The front of the
case shows a profile bust of *Queen
Elizabeth I*, the back the *Ark of the
English Church tossed on a stormy sea.*
Height 7 cm
Inv.no.M81-1935

5
German (Augsburg), 1584
Astronomical globe
Bronze gilt. Made for the *Kunstkammer*
of Emperor Rudolph II (1576-1612) in
Prague by Georg Roll and Johannes
Reinhold. Height 42 cm
Inv.no.246-1865

1

3

The intricate skill and precision of the metalworker's art is demonstrated in the 16th-century Renaissance metalwork collections. The Burghley nef is one of the few pieces of 16th-century French plate in the collection and one of the most remarkable survivals anywhere. Designed to contain the salt, its position on the high-table at a banquet marked the honour due to the more distinguished guests.

The astronomical globe made for Emperor Rudolph II is one of a series cast in bronze from the same moulds. It bears witness to the remarkable technical skill of late 16th-century German instrument makers and bronze founders. Although primarily designed as a precise mathematical instrument, great attention has been paid to the visual effect of the piece. The legs are embellished with Renaissance ornament of flowers and animal feet interpreted in a typically flamboyant style.

4

6

6
English (London), 1525
The Howard Grace cup (also known as the Thomas-a-Becket cup)
Ivory bowl and cover, mounted in silver gilt and set with garnets and pearls. Height 30.2 cm
Inv.no.M2680-1932

5

1

3

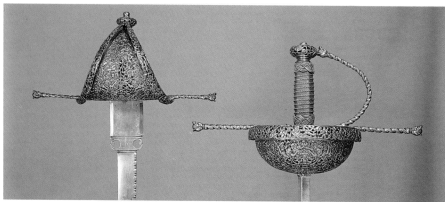

2

1
English (London), 1588
Clock
Gilt brass case. Engraved with foliage
and monsters after designs by Nicaise
Roussel. Signed by François Nowe
and dated. Height 33 cm
Inv.no.M39-1959

2
Italian (Naples), 1650
Rapier and dagger
Chiselled and pierced steel. Made by
Antonio Cilenta. Rapier; length
114.3 cm; dagger; length 59.7 cm
Inv.nos.M56-1947, M124-1921

3
English (London), 1592
The Vyvyan salt
Silver gilt chased and set with panels
and medallions of *verre eglomisé*.
Surmounted by a figure of *Justice*, and
decorated with emblems and
medallions bearing heads of *Ninus*,
Cyrus, *Alexander* and *Julius Caesar*.
Height 34 cm
Inv.no.M273-1925
The Vyvyan salt is so named from the
Vyvyans of Trelowarren, Cornwall,
who owned it since the 16th century.
It is among the most important
surviving pieces of English 16th-
century court goldsmith's work. The
form of the salt resembles that of
contemporary clocks, the dome
shaped cover echoing the bell on
which the hours were struck. The
panels of *verre eglomisé* on the base
show floral patterns taken directly
from designs in Geoffrey Whitney's *A
Choice of Emblems* published in 1586.
The use of costly materials and
exquisite workmanship indicate that
the Vyvyan salt was intended for a
patron of considerable means.

4
French (Blois), *c*1640
Watch
Silver and gilt brass (with modern
silver additions to the case). Signed
'N. Lemmaindre A Blois'. Length
7.6 cm, width 2.8 cm
Inv.no.M132-1923

5
French or the Netherlandish, *c*1630
Breast ornament
Gold, enamelled and set with table-cut
and facetted point-cut diamonds.
Height 12.4 cm, width 7.4 cm
Inv.no.M143-1975

6
Netherlandish (Utrecht), 1612
Tazza
Silver chased, with an embossed scene
of the *Judgement of Solomon* on the
bowl. Signed by Adam van Vianen.
Height 16.5 cm, diameter 20.3 cm
Inv.no.2125-1855

4

5

6

1
German (Augsburg), c1700
Monstrance
Silver and parcel gilt. Decorated with
the *Last Supper* on the front; figures of
Faith, Hope and *Charity* on the stem;

and on the base, scenes of the
Crucifixion, the *Adoration of the Magi,*
Mary Magdalen washing Christ's feet,
and the *Arrival of the Magi.* Height
99.1 cm
Inv.no.M3-1952

2
English, 18th century
Trivet
Wrought iron, 40 × 33.6 cm
Inv.no.580-1905

1

2

3
English (London), 1683
The Calverley toilet service
Silver, chased and cast with scenes
from classical mythology and foliage
after Guglielmo della Porta. Mirror
57.2 × 37.5 cm
Inv.nos.240-1879 to 240m-1879
This toilet service was bought second-
hand as a wedding gift for Lady
Calverley in 1707. It comprises a
mirror frame, a pair of standing dishes,
a pair of caskets, a pair of circular
boxes, a pair of low vases and a
pincushion. It was customary for
wealthy brides to receive such highly
ornamented toilet services as wedding
presents from their bridegrooms
during the period between roughly
1640 and 1780.

3

4

5

6

4
English (London), 1743
The Newdigate centrepiece
Silver, cast and chased with flowers, busts and country scenes, including the arms of Newdigate impaling Conyers. An inscription states that it was the gift of the Rt Hon. Sophia Baroness Lempster to Sir Roger and Lady Newdigate on their wedding in 1743. Made by Paul de Lamerie. Height 23 cm, width 2 cm
Inv.no.M149-1919

5
English, (London) 1698
Pair of waiters
Silver gilt with chased ornament, including the arms of Sir William de Courtenay of Powderham Castle, Devon. Goldsmith's mark of Benjamin Pyne. Diameter 24 cm
Inv.nos.M77-1947, M77A-1947

6
English (London), 1773
Pair of sauceboats
Silver, chased. Engraved with arms of Sir Watkin Williams Wynn. Designed by Robert Adam. Goldsmith's mark of John Carter. Height 13.7 cm
Inv.nos.M13-1987, M13a-1987

1
French (Paris), 1788
Firegrate and pair of columns
Gilt bronze. Signed 'Thomire A Paris'
(Pierre-Philippe Thomire), and dated.
Grate, height 84.5 cm, width 109.5 cm;
columns, height, 105 cm
Inv.nos.M19a-1987, M19b-1987

2
English (London), 1802
The Islington cup
Silver, parcel gilt. Shows a shield cast
with the arms of Alexander Aubert,
the recipient, and on the back an
engraved shield surmounted by a
figure of *Fame* with an inscription
stating that it was presented by the
late Corps of the Loyal Islington
Volunteers. Designed by John
Thurston. Modelled by Edmund
Coffin. Height 49 cm
Inv.nos.M12-1987 to M12b-1987

3
French (Paris), 1775
Snuff-box
Gold, enamelled and set with panels
of lapis lazuli and miniatures under
glass. Goldsmith's mark of Pierre
François Drais. On the lid is a
miniature group portrait of Queen
Marie Antoinette and three of her
children, Marie Thérèse Charlotte, the
Dauphin Louis, and Louis Joseph
Xavier François. On the base a
miniature depicts the Comte de
Provence (later Louis XVIII), the
Comte d'Artois (later Charles X) and
Madame Elisabeth. 7.6 × 5.5 cm
Inv.no.905-1882; Jones collection

4
English, 1835-45
Necklace
Gold set with seed pearls forming
clusters of grapes, length 59.7 cm
Inv.no.M133-1951

5
English (London), 1862
The Royal Order of Victoria and
Albert
Onyx cameo with busts of Queen
Victoria and the Prince Consort,
surrounded by border of brilliants and
pastes and surmounted by an imperial
crown of diamonds, rubies and
emeralds. Cameo signed by Tommaso
Saulini of Rome (1793-1864). The
Order made by Garrards of Panton
Street. Height 8.8 cm, width 4.3 cm
Inv.no.M180-1976

6
English (London), mid-19th century
Wine flagon in the Islamic style
Silver, parcel gilt, decorated with
embossed and chased work.
Made by C. T. and G. Fox for Lambert
& Rawlings. Height 60.5 cm
Purchased from the Great Exhibition
in 1851; inv.no.2743-1851

1

2

3

4

5

6

8

7

9

Silver, height 12 cm, width 10 cm
Inv.no.371-1865
A reissue of a design byRichard
Redgrave c1849. In this piece
Redgrave's literal application of the
Summerly ideas on 'appropriate'
motifs produced a shape which was
hard for a child to drink from.

7
English (Birmingham), 1883
The Jasmine vase
Silver mounted with steel plaques
inlaid with coloured golds, silver,
copper. Designed by August Willms.
Manufactured by Elkington & Co.
Height 51.9 cm
Inv.no.M84-1987

8
North American (New York),
***c*1878-90**
Coffee service, comprising coffee-pot,
creamer and sugar bowl
Silver, inlaid with various metals.

Made by Tiffany and Co. Coffee-pot,
height 20.5 cm; creamer, height 7 cm;
sugar bowl, height 5.5 cm
Inv.no.M26-1970

9
Richard Redgrave (1804-88)
English
'Guardian Angel' christening mug,
1865-66
Hallmarks for London 1865-6; maker's
mark for Harry Emmanuel
Originally made by S. H. & D. Gass for
Summerley Art Manufactures in 1849
and exhibited at the Great Exhibition
of 1851

Many of the metalwork objects in the
collections combine various metals,
some precious, others base,
juxtaposed for contrasting visual
effect. The Jasmine vase is a good
example of silver intricately combined
with other metals. Its body is
composed of two oval panels of steel
inlaid with coloured golds, silver and
copper in *japonaiserie* style with birds,
plants and insects, including a spider
in its web. These panels are set in
frames of silver with a pair of putti
flying from flowers on either side. The
quatrefoil foot of the base is also
composed of steel panels mounted in
silver and decorated with inlaid
insects and blossoms, and around the
base of the foot with a stylised border
of foliage and flowers and two
squirrels. The exterior of the neck has
a steel collar beneath further inlaid
panels, with a female face in silver
mounted on each side, whilst the
interior is silver gilt. On top, an eagle
perched on a ball surmounts the
stopper.

1
English, c1880
Soup tureen and ladle
Electroplate. Designed by Christopher
Dresser. Manufactured by Hukin &
Heath (Birmingham and London).
Tureen, height 21.6 cm, diameter
23.5 cm; ladle length, 35 cm
Inv.nos.M26-1972 to M26b-1972

2
English (Birmingham), 1903
Casket
Silver, decorated with embossed work
and cabuchon opals. Designed by
Archibald Knox. Manufactured by
W. H. Haseler. 11.2 × 21.5 × 13 cm
Inv.no.M15-1970

3
English (London), 1988
Brooch in the form of a fishhead
Conserved red bream head, gold leaf,
glass eye, resin, watercolour and
enamel paint. Designed and made by
Simon Costin. Height 7.9 cm, width
13 cm
Inv.no.M61-1988

1

2

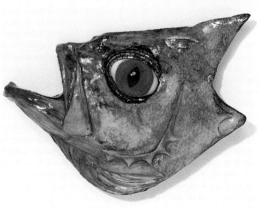

3

4

5

The Metalwork Collection is continually being enriched with purchases from contemporary metalworkers and jewellers, many of whom employ unusual and unconventional materials and methods. The fish-head brooch commissioned from Simon Costin, a taxidermist, theatre designer and metalworker, in 1987 is one such example. It makes use of a red bream head, dried and preserved with formaldehyde before being lined with 18 ct gold and decorated with a taxidermist's glass eye for a puma, Venetian glass beads, enamel paint and watercolour. The entire head was then coated with polyurethane varnish. Since the first completed head was eaten by rats in Simon Costin's workshop, the Museum's brooch is technically a replica of the original piece.

4
German (Weimar), 1924
Table lamp 'MT8'
Nickel-plated brass and milk-glass. Designed and made by Wilhelm Wagenfeld at the Bauhaus. Height 28 cm
Inv.nos.M28-1989, M28a-1989

5
German (Weimar), 1923
Ashtray
Brass and nickel-silver alloy. Designed and made by Marianne Brandt at the Bauhaus. Height 6.7 cm, width 9.9 cm
Inv.no.M73-1988

6
English (London), 1980
Pair of candelabra
Silver. Goldsmith's mark of Robert Welch. Commissioned by the Museum for its permanent collections. Height 38 cm, width 31.5 cm
Inv.nos.M61-1980, M61a-1980

7
German, 1980
Grille
Wrought mild steel. Designed and made by Klaus Walz. Height 230 cm, width 120 cm
Inv.no.M947-1983

8
North American, 1988
Brooch: *The Virgin and the unicorn*
Gold, 'oxidised' silver, *cloisonné* enamel on silver, pearls, lead and amethyst. Designed and made by William Harper. Height 16.5 cm, width 7.6 cm
Inv.no.M3-1990

6

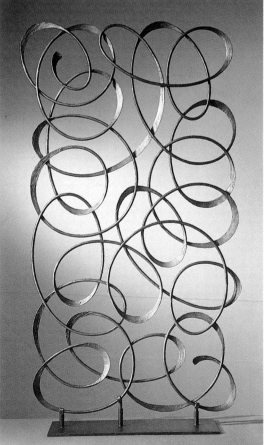

7

8

The East Asian Collections

The Far Eastern section of the Museum holds about sixty thousand works of art which have come from China, Korea and Japan. The material in this book mirrors the arrangement of the four major galleries in which this collection is displayed. The largest gallery is the T. T. Tsui Gallery of Chinese Art, which was re-opened after complete refurbishment in 1991. Nearby are rooms which contain the Toshiba Gallery of Japanese Art, and the Gallery of Chinese Export Art made possible by Gerald Godfrey, which were inaugurated in 1986 and 1987 respectively. The adjacent Samsung Gallery of Korean Art will open at the end of 1992.

China

As early as the neolithic period (about 5000-1700 BC) Chinese people were interring beautiful objects with their dead. Many of the fine early jades and pots in the Museum's collection are the sort of precious objects found in graves. By 2000 BC large pierced cylinders and circles of jade were being worked to a remarkable degree of precision, given the limits of Stone Age technology. The objects shown on p.109 are tall, hollow cylinders of jade called in Chinese *cong*. They were ritual items that seem to have had some special associations with the *shamans* or religious leaders of the communities. The first historic culture of China, that of the Shang state, emerged about 1700 BC. In this, the Bronze Age, metal was the prime signifier of wealth, and fine bronzes like that on p.109 were placed in sets in the tombs of kings and powerful nobles.

By the time of the Han dynasty (206 BC-AD 220) tomb art included wall paintings and extensive sculpted reliefs in which legend and daily life are depicted in an extremely realistic manner, as they are also in the sets of pottery models placed there to accompany the dead (p.109). Jade was an important item in Han dynasty funeral art (p.109). There followed a period of disunity and war, which came to an end in the late sixth century and was followed by the expansionist Tang dynasty (618-906). Enough survives of the arts of Tang China to demonstrate its abundant prosperity, power and self-confidence as the leading world force of its day. Lavish tomb furnishings included boldly modelled animals (p.110). Splendid silver and gold vessels survive, as well as translucent white porcelain which was made for the first time (p.110). The development of classic Chinese ceramics in the following Song period (960-1278) included the production of bluish-green Ru and Guan imperial wares with their characteristic crackled glazes (p.112).

The Yuan dynasty of the Mongols (1279-1368) was deeply resented in China, and many refused to serve it. It was a time of new departures in painting and ceramics; the invention of underglaze blue-painted porcelain exactly suited the taste for pictorial design and extrovert colour (p.119). The building of the Forbidden City in Peking in the early Ming dynasty (1368-1644) set a new architectural standard, complemented in the crafts by plain, elegant furniture and resplendent lacquerwork (p.113). Silk textiles such as the fine tapestry *kesi* were used in both furnishings and dress.

1
Chinese (Neolithic), *c*2800-1900 BC
Three *cong* or cylinders
Jade, height 40.3, 43.2 and 20.4 cm
Inv.nos.A40-1936, A46-1936, A50-1936

3
Han dynasty, between 206 BC and AD 220
Horse's head
Jade, height 14 cm
Inv.no.A16-1935

2
Han dynasty, between 206 BC and AD 220
A woman and a dog
Ceramic, painted and glazed, woman, height 49.6 cm; dog, length 34.9 cm
Inv.nos.C924-1935, C167-1914

4
Shang dynasty, *c*1200-1100 BC
Zun or vessel in the shape of an owl
Bronze, height 21 cm
Inv.no.M5-1935

1

2

3

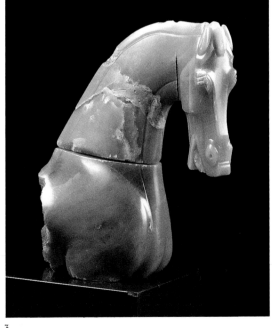

4

1
Tang dynasty, c700-50
Horse
Ceramic with lead glazes, height
74.1 cm
Inv.no.c50-1964

2
**Sui, Tang and Five dynasties,
between 580 and 950**
Vessels
Silver and porcelain, maximum height
7.6 cm
Inv.nos.CIRC5-1933, C138-1965,
FE34-1973, M35-1935

3
Jin dynasty, c1200
The Bodhissatva Guanyin
Wood, painted, lacquered and gilt,
height 96.4 cm
Inv.no.A7-1935
When this magnificent sculpture was
conserved by the Museum's
Conservation Department, it was
found that the figure had been
completely redecorated four times.
When Guanyin was newly made, he
was painted in a naturalistic manner,
with pink flesh, blue-black hair, and
red, blue, green and gold silk robes.
At some time in the Ming dynasty
(1368-1644) the image was restored,
the flesh painted red-gold and the
robes gold with an embossed surface.
The figure then resembled a gilt-
bronze statue. This gilt-bronze
appearance was refurbished once
more, and then, finally, the surface
was reinforced with a paper layer and
repainted. This last, garish restoration
probably took place shortly before the
piece was sold on the international art
market in the early 20th century. The
conservators removed the top layer of
paper and paint to reveal the gilt-
bronze-like surface applied in the
Ming dynasty; there was not enough
of the original, Jin dynasty surface left
to present an attractive appearance.

1

2

3

1

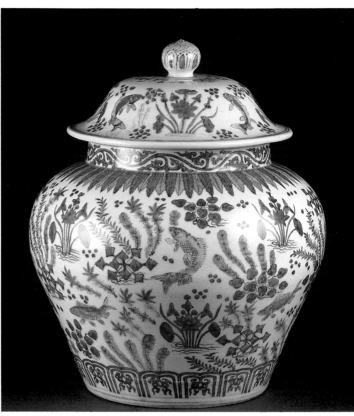

2

4

1

Northern Song, Southern Song and Qing (Yongzheng period) dynasties, respectively 960-1127, 1128-1279 and 1723-35
Cupstand of Ru ware (Northern Song); lobed bowl of Guan ware (Southern Song); vase of imitation Guan ware (Qing)
Lobed bowl, diameter 16.5 cm; cupstand, height 9.9 cm; vase, height 20.7 cm
Inv.nos.FE1-1970, C25-1935, 1846-1888

2

Yuan dynasty, c1320-50
Blue-and-white vase
Porcelain, height 35.9 cm
Inv.no.c8-1952

3

Ming dynasty (Jiajing reign), between 1522 and 1566
Blue-and-white jar and lid
Ceramic, glazed and painted in red over the glaze (the fishes), height 40.6 cm
Inv.no.CIRC118-1936

4

Qing dynasty, c1650-1700
Kesi or tapestry hanging
Silk, height 198 cm
Inv.no.T844-1919

5

Ming dynasty, c1550-1600
Two armchairs
Huali wood, height 102.9 cm
Inv.nos.FE54-1977, FE55-1977; given by Sir John Addis

6

Ming dynasty (Xuande period), 1426-35
Table
Carved lacquer on a wood core, height 79.2 cm
Inv.no.FE6-1973
This unique treasure is a remarkably rare survival. It has three equal-sized drawers beneath its top surface, and carries an imperial reign mark of the Xuande period (1426-35). The dating is confirmed by the clear connection of the dragons, phoenixes and flowers which cover its surface to the decoration of smaller objects from the same period. The table is unique not only for its decoration but for its shape, and it may well have been made in a workshop under direct imperial control. The workshop could even have been Peking's famous 'Orchard Workshop', which was

established soon after the transfer of the capital to northern China in 1421. The table may have left an imperial palace some time ago, for the five-clawed dragons carved on its surface, which suggest imperial provenance, have been mutilated by the removal of one claw on each foot.

5

6

1

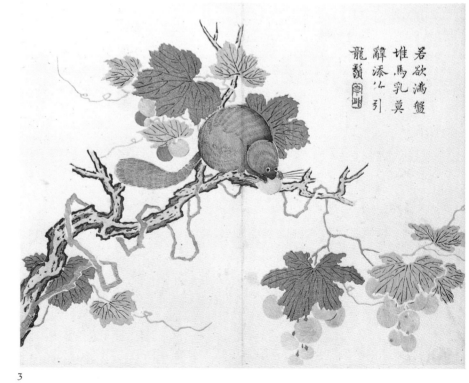

2

3

1
Qing dynasty (Kangxi and Yongzheng periods, respectively 1622-1722 and 1723-35)
Dish and bowl of imperial ware
Porcelain, respectively 25.5 cm and 9 cm in diameter
Inv.nos.C3-1947 and 644-1907;
Gulland gift

2
Qing dynasty, c1700
Cup and stand
Rhinoceros horn and carved wood, total height 15.9 cm
Inv.no.162-1879

3
Wang Gai (active c1679-1705)
Page from *The Mustard Seed Garden Manual of Painting*, Part III, 1701
Woodblock print, 30.5 × 37.3 cm
Inv.no.E4779-1916; Alexander gift

4
Qing dynasty, 19th century
Manchu woman's robe with characters for 'double happiness'
Silk, tapestry weave, 140 × 205 cm
Inv.no.T233-1948

5
Qing dynasty (Qianlong period), between 1736 and 1795
Nest of boxes
Lacquer, height 25.4 cm
Inv.no.FE65-1974; made for the imperial court

4

5

China and Chinese Export Art

Under the Qing dynasty (1644-1911) a wide variety of crafts were consumed by a populace that was growing in both numbers and wealth. It was during this time that trade in craft goods with Europe developed, and many items in western museums represent articles made in China for foreign customers. The difference in forms and styles of decoration can be observed by comparing the Qing dynasty art works on pp.112–115, which were made for the domestic market, and those on pp. 116-117 which were made for export.

1

1

Chinese, 1780-83
The Canton waterfront
Watercolour on silk, 53.3 × 32.4 cm
Inv.no.D448-1887

2

Chinese, c1730
Decorated chair
Wood overlaid with gold and black lacquer, the seat of lacquered leather stuffed with horsehair, height 100 cm
Inv.no.FE116-1978

3

Chinese, c1820-40
Pendant of concentric balls
Ivory, length 45.7 cm
Inv.no.380-1872

2

3

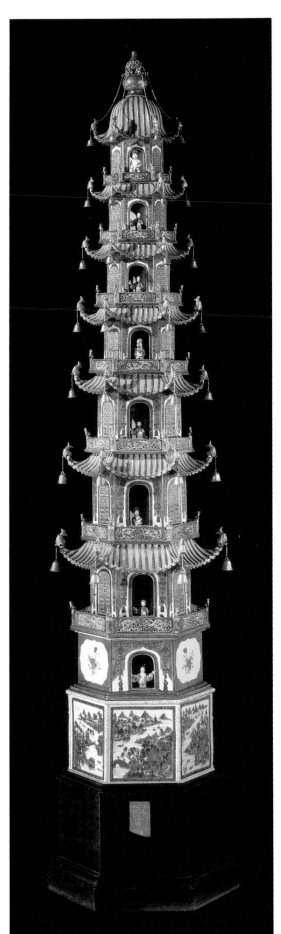

4

Chinese, c1800-15
Pagoda
Porcelain with underglaze blue and
other colours overglaze, height
276 cm
Inv.no.c80-1954

5

Chinese, c1770
A loom width of painted silk
Painted silk, 84 × 76 cm
Inv.no.τ121-1933; Deedes gift

4

5

117

Korea

The Korean people are ethnically and linguistically distinct from their Chinese neighbours, and although their country stands as a geographical bridge between China and Japan, their culture has developed along its own distinctive lines. The Museum has a few examples of early Korean art, but is better represented in the highly developed crafts of the Koryŏ dynasty (918-1392). The serenely graceful painted Buddhist hanging scroll of *Samantabadhra on an elephant* (p.119) and the rare inlaid bronze vase (p.118) reflect the sophistication of the period. The flowering of Koryŏ culture is nowhere more fully shown than in ceramics, where a celadon-glazed ware was produced that for refinement of design, nobility of form, and a gently glowing brilliance of glaze was acknowledged to be outstanding even by the contemporary Song Chinese (pp.118–119). After the Mongol invasion which devastated the country in the thirteenth century, the Chosŏn dynasty was founded, remaining in power from 1392 to 1910. In pottery, an innate artistry shines through in wares which, although sometimes roughly and even crudely made, display an outstanding vigour and expressive power (p.119).

1
Koryŏ dynasty, c1100-1200
Vase
Bronze inlaid with silver wire, height 25 cm
Inv.no.M1189-1926

2
Koryŏ dynasty, c1100-50
Vase with lotus pattern
Ceramic, with pattern incised under celadon green glaze, height 34.1 cm
Inv.no.c70-1935

3
Koryŏ dynasty, c1250-1350
Bodhisattva Samantabadhra
Colours and gold on silk, 139 × 56 cm
Inv.no.FE51-1976

4
Koryŏ dynasty, c1150-1250
Vase with black and white decoration
Ceramic, with celadon green glaze, inlays in black and white slip and copper red painting, height 34.6 cm
Inv.no.c72-1911

5
Chosŏn dynasty, c1650-1750
Jar with lotus pattern
Porcelain with pattern drawn in underglaze red, height 28.9 cm
Inv.no.c131-1913

1

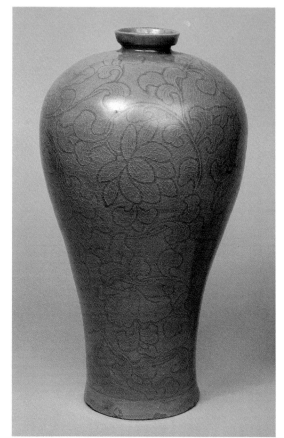

2

3

4

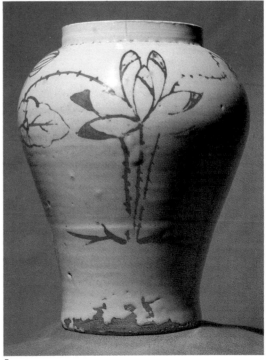

5

Japan

The native culture of Japan was influenced by the introduction of Buddhism from Korea at the Asuka court (552-645), while in the Nara period (645-794) contact was maintained with the Chinese Tang dynasty court. Chinese influence can be observed in the development of ceramics, the tall-necked Sue ware jar (p.121) taking its form from imported Chinese bronzes, for example. The Heian court (794-1185), established at modern Kyoto, presided over a learned and sophisticated society; and the military leaders of the period of Kamakura rule (1185-1333) also became worthy patrons. Throughout this period, Buddhist sculpture and painting were extremely refined and expressive (pp.120–121).

Chanoyu, or the tea ceremony as it is often called, developed into basic forms still recognisable today during the 16th and 17th centuries. Tea utensils were recorded in specially compiled catalogues of art treasures, and pieces with rough, naturalistic qualities were juxtaposed with more smoothly crafted wares for a powerful aesthetic effect (p.121).

From the 17th century, Japan started to produce porcelain, and to export craft goods to the west in the same manner as the Chinese. The development of lacquer as a luxury art had begun in Nara times, with the Japanese outstripping even the Chinese in invention and skill. Contact with foreign countries is recorded in a colourful screen recording the arrival of a European ship (pp.122-123), while the lavishly decorated box illustrated on p.123 was made to order for an official of the Dutch East India Company.

Items made for the domestic market reached heights of technical excellence in the Edo period (1615-1868), as the elegant porcelain dish (p.122) and the woodblock print (p.124) indicate. *Ukiyo-e* woodblock printing of pictures and illustrated books had been flourishing for 200 years when westerners, arriving in the 1850s and 1860s, disclosed the extraordinary richness of this Japanese tradition to the outside world. So complex and inventive are their images, that ever since then Japanese prints have been avidly sought by collectors throughout the world.

The museum's holdings of the late 19th- and 20-century arts, already considerable, are being further extended by an active programme to acquire contemporary pieces (p. 127).

1
Late Heian period, *c*1100-85
Boddhisattva Seishi
Colours on silk, 1002 × 56.8 cm
Inv.no.FE105-1970

2
Nara period, *c*675-750
Tall-necked jar of Sue ware
Stoneware with green ash glaze, height 27.4 cm
Inv.no.FE7-1972

1

120

2

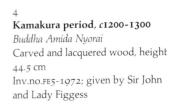

3
Meiji period, c1900
Vase
Cloisonné enamel, height 31 cm
Inv.no.265-1903

4
Kamakura period, c1200-1300
Buddha Amida Nyorai
Carved and lacquered wood, height
44.5 cm
Inv.no.FE5-1972; given by Sir John
and Lady Figgess

4

5

5
Momoyama period, 1590-1630
Tea ceremony utensils
Ceramic. Raku tea bowl attributed to
Hon'ami Kōetsu, diameter 12.7 cm;

Karatsu freshwater jar, height 10.6 cm;
Bizen tea caddy with ivory lid, height
7.3 cm
Inv.nos.247-1877, FE10-1972,
189-1877

1

Momoyama period, *c*1600-25
Six-fold screen: *The arrival of European traders in Japan*
Colours and gilding on paper,
367 × 160 cm
Inv.no.803-1892

2

Edo period, *c*1700-25
Dish of Nabeshima ware
Porcelain with underglaze blue and
overglaze colours, diameter 20.3 cm
Inv.no.352-1877

3

Edo period, 1636-39
The Van Diemen box (view of top)
Wood with black, gold, silver and red
lacquer decoration, and gold and
silver details, length 48 cm
Inv.no.w49-1916; given by the
children of Sir Trevor Lawrence, Bart.

2

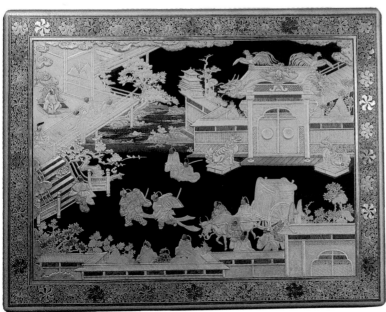

The document box takes its name
from Maria Van Diemen, wife of the
Governor-General of the Dutch East
Indies from 1636 to 1645, whose
name is inscribed in gold inside the
lid. The box stands out from other
lacquers of the period made for export
to Europe because of its shape, which
is Japanese rather than European. Such
rectangular boxes, measuring about
45 × 30 cm and used to hold writing
paper, were one of several practical
new shapes first made during the
Momoyama period. The decoration
on the lid shows scenes from chapters
1 and 7 of the 11th-century novel *Tale
of Genji*. In chapter 1, the young
Prince Genji's coming-of-age
ceremony is described, and here he is
seen about to mount the steps of a
palace where the Emperor sits with his
ministers, just as in the story.

3

1

Edo period, *c*1790–1800
Sunrise
Woodblock print by Eishōsai Chōki,
height 38.7 cm
Inv.no.E3774-1953

2

Meiji period, 1904
*Japanese destroyers engage a Russian
battleship*
Woodblock print, by Tsukioka Kōgyo,
length 76.2 cm
Inv.no.E3140-1905

3

Edo period, *c*1850
Woman's kimono
Green satin-weave silk with
embroidered decoration, 189 × 124 cm
Inv.no.FE11-1983

1

2

Loose straight-seamed garments worn crossed-over in front from left to right are the traditional clothes of Japan for both men and women. The term used for them is *kimono*, which translates as 'the thing worn'. It is clear from Japanese woodblock prints that fashion in kimonos was a matter of both decoration and cut. This was achieved not by accentuating a particular part of the body, but rather by emphasizing the drape of the robe at collar and hem. A woman's neck could be made to appear more slender and graceful by careful arrangement of the collar and by styling the hair in upswept piles. Female kimonos were also much longer than the height of a human figure, for they were worn with elevated wooden pattens (*geta*), and often swept the ground. The decoration of this kimono, in gold work and polychrome embroidery in untwisted silk, is of extremely high quality.

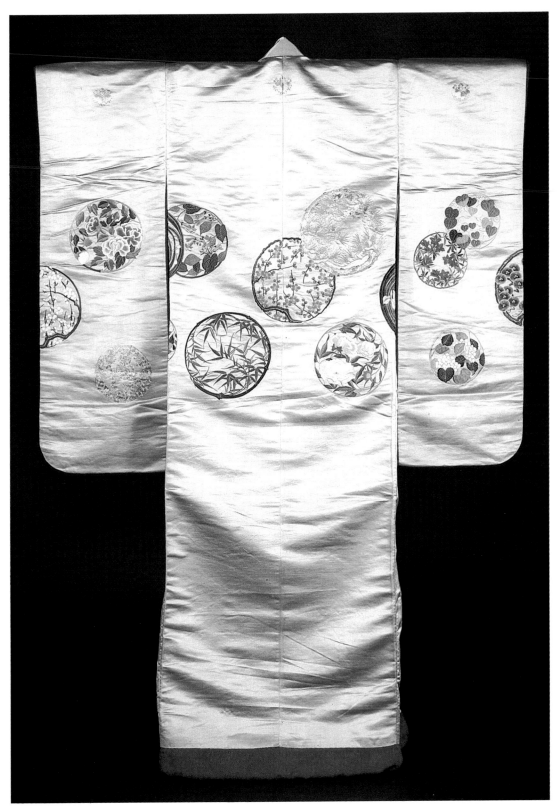

3

1
Edo period, 1859
Suit of armour in Ōyoroi style
Helmet of iron with gilt fittings,
signed 'made by Myochin Mondo Ki
no Muneharu on a day in the 8th
month of the 6th year of Ansei'
(1859); mask of iron with whiskers of
animal hair; small-plates of gold-
lacquered iron and leather, laced with
silk; sleeves and leg-guards of iron;
breast-plate, shoulder-strap protectors
and other details of stencilled leather;
sleeves of patterned silk; trimmings of
gilt openwork; cords of red silk; boots
of stencilled leather, gilt and fur,
height as shown 146 cm Inv.no.362
-1865; given by Queen Victoria

2

1

2
**Edo period, late 18th and 19th
centuries**
Three *inro* or carrying containers,
attached to *netsuke* or belt toggles

Lacquered wood, maximum height
8.3 cm
Inv.nos.W145-1922, W221-1922,
W284-1922; all Pfungst gift

3

3
Meiji period, c1900
Vase
Cloisonné enamel, height 31 cm
Inv.no.265-1903

4
Isaburō Kado (born 1940)
Tray, 1985
Lacquer on a wood core, width
60.5 cm
Inv.no.FE2-1986

5
Kazuo Takiguchi (born 1953)
Vessel, 1988
Glazed stoneware, length 78 cm
Inv.no.FE15-1989

4

These large and splendid examples of contemporary Japanese ceramics and lacquerware are just two of a number of recent purchases made by the Museum in the field of modern Japanese studio crafts. Kado is a native of Wajima in northern central Japan, where there has been an important lacquer industry since the 18th century. He has a more spontaneous approach to the making of lacquer than many of his contemporaries, and in this piece explores the subtle changes of colour that occur across the sharp edges and angles of the boldly geometric form. Takiguchi is an important figure in a new generation of young Japanese avantgarde ceramic artists. He has been the recipient of several prestigious awards in recent years. He achieves his expansive but monumental forms through a remarkable technique which involves draping a huge sheet of very thin clay over a loosely formed mould and deftly cutting and joining it into the intended shape. His work is also interesting in that it is almost invariably created for a particular space, specific forms being determined by the overall installation plan he has in mind.

5

The Indian, Himalayan and South-East Asian Collections

The Indian, Himalayan and South-East Asian collections contain objects from the countries of the Indian subcontinent (India, Pakistan, Bangladesh, Sri Lanka), together with Afghanistan, the Himalayan regions of Tibet, Nepal and Bhutan, and mainland and insular South-East Asia (Burma, Thailand, Kampuchea, Vietnam, Malaysia and Indonesia). The early traditions of the Indian subcontinent, represented largely by stone and metal sculptures, are presented in the Indian Sculpture Gallery, together with the arts of the Himalayas and South-East Asia. The arts of India from the beginning of the Mughal period until the close of the nineteenth century are displayed in the Nehru Gallery of Indian art.

The Indian subcontinent, an area as large and as culturally diverse as Europe, has produced through its village artisans, its centres of specialist production and its imperial workshops an immense range and wealth of art. The Museum houses the largest and finest collection of Indian decorative arts, assembled from the end of the eighteenth century when the virtues of Indian arts were first widely appreciated in the West.

It is difficult now fully to appreciate the scale of the artistic achievements of classical India. The sculptures which survive in stone, bronze, terracotta, stucco, ivory and wood provide us with some of the finest images produced in the service of religion. Sculptures dedicated to Hindu, Buddhist and Jain deities were produced in workshops under both noble and religious patronage.

With the ascendancy of a succession of Muslim dynasties in northern India and the Deccan from the thirteenth century, the predominantly Hindu character of Indian culture came increasingly under threat. The arrival of the Mughals and their establishment of an empire in India in the sixteenth century marked a turning point, bringing with them elements of Iranian and Central Asian culture. The Mughals progressively extended their control over the subcontinent in the late sixteenth and seventeenth century, and the courtly arts of the subcontinent came increasingly under the influence of the Mughal imperial style. By the eighteenth century however, the empire was disintegrating. Many of the emerging regional kingdoms were, in turn, subjugated by the European trading companies, most notably by the English East India Company, and elements of European taste were adopted in some of these courts. British control passed from the Company to the government after the Indian rebellion of 1857, instituting the era of the Raj, which lasted until Indian independence was declared in 1947. The Museum's collection continues to reflect contemporary Indian artistic developments in the acquisition of twentieth-century painting, sculpture and decorative arts.

Hindu, Buddhist and Jain India

The arts of ancient and mediaeval India were largely created in the service of religion and survive mainly in the form of temples and shrines, together with the sculptures and painting used to decorate them. The relic mounds (stupas) which mark early Buddhist sites, such as Sanchi and Bharhut, were decorated with richly carved stone railings and ornamental gateways (toranas). Few free-standing temples predate the 6th century, but earlier rock-cut shrines, as seen at Ajanta, contain in their interiors elaborate sculpture programmes and the remains of splendid wall paintings. Literary sources inform us that painting on cloth was widely practised, for both secular and religious use, but nothing survives from this early period. The earliest illustrated manuscripts, on palm-leaf, date from around the 12th century.

Sculpture in India has its beginnings in early terracotta female figurines and stone images of nature-spirits (yakshan). By about the 1st century BC figurative sculptures of deities belonging to the major religions of the subcontinent began to appear. In the following centuries artists worked for all communities, Hindu, Buddhist and Jain, producing innovative sculptures which reflected the growing complexity of Indian religious iconography. It was an art intimately associated with the ritual life of the temple, the sculptures being intended both to honour the deity and to be a means by which the faithful, through ritual and prayer, could seek the deity's protection and benevolence.

1
South India (probably Nagapattinam), 11th-12th century
The Buddha
Gilt bronze, height 68.6 cm
Inv.no.IPN2639
This sculpture is one of the finest Buddhist bronzes to survive from South India. Buddhism came early to southern India, as recorded by the 3rd century BC inscriptions of Emperor Aśoka. The region continued to be a centre of Buddhist learning as late as the 12th century, despite the growing dominance of Hinduism.

1

1
North Indian (Mathura), Kushan dynasty, 2nd century
Yakshī (tree spirit)
Height 51 cm
Inv.no.IM72-1927
Yakshī were animistic nature-spirits belonging to early Indian cults which were absorbed into Buddhist and Jain worship as images of fertility.

2
Pakistani (Taxila?), Kushan dynasty, *c*2nd century
Pendant with the goddess *Hariti*
Gold repoussé, with garnet and pearls, height 4.5 cm
Inv.no.IS9-1948

3
Eastern Indian, late 11th or early 12th century
Stone Buddha
Height 125 cm
Inv.no.617-1872
The Buddha, wearing the crown and ornaments of a monarch, makes the sign of touching the earth as a witness to his Enlightenment.

1

2

3

4

6

4
Afghanistan (probably Hadda), 4th-5th century
Head of the Buddha
Lime plaster with traces of pigment, height 24.75 cm
Inv.no.IM3-1931
This gracious head in the Gandhara style has the sacred marks of the Buddha: a prominant hair-knot (*usnisa*), forehead mark (*urna*) and elongated earlobes. Much of the Greco-Roman influence apparent in earlier Gandharan sculpture is still to be seen in this stucco head, despite the prevailing influence of the Gupta style by this period.

5

5
Kashmir (Harwan), 4th-5th century
Two ascetics
Terracotta tile with moulded relief, inscribed in Kharoshthi script, height 53.4 cm
Inv.no.IS9-1978
This tile served as a bench riser around a courtyard at the Buddhist monastery of Harwan.

6
Central Indian (Sanchi), c900
The Bodhisattva Avalokiteśvara
Sandstone, height 86.4 cm
Inv.no.IM184-1910
The 'Sanchi torso' was discovered in 1883 during excavation of portions of the western gateway (*torana*) of Stūpa No.1 at Sanchi. Its precise identification remained ambiguous until 1971.

1

1

South Deccan, late 16th–early 17th century
Nandi, Śiva's sacred bull
Serpentine(?)
Height 64.8 cm, length 82.6 cm
Inv.no.IS73-1990
In a Hindu temple dedicated to the worship of Śiva, the presence of the bull-calf Nandi is essential. Nandi is Śiva's *vāhana* or sacred vehicle and is traditionally positioned in the temple courtyard facing directly into the central sanctuary which houses the principal Śiva image, the *linga*. The Sanskrit word *nandi* means 'joy' and refers to the emotions experienced by a devotee in the presence of Lord Śiva.

2

Tamilnadu, 11th century
Śiva Nataraja
Bronze, height 89 cm
Inv.no.IM2-1934
Ringed by a circle of flames, Śiva as 'Lord of the Dance' dances on the back of the prostrate dwarf Apasmara, who signifies the power of ignorance and materialism. In two of his hands he carries the drum and a tongue of flame, symbolizing the complementary universal principles of Creation and Destruction. His two lower hands make the gesture of protection and point to his raised left foot, the worship of which leads to salvation.

3

Western Indian, 9th–10th century
Jina (Jain Saviour)
Bronze, height 25 cm
Inv.no.IS10-1968
In keeping with the ascetic and world-denying tenor of Jainism, images of the 24 Jain Saviours tend to be hieratically formal in character, and to lack the sensuousness and elegance of much Indian figure sculpture. They are usually shown as standing or seated ascetics, absorbed in profound meditation.

4

2

3

4

Eastern Indian (Orissa), Eastern Gangā dynasty, c1100
The Mother-goddess Ambikā
Stone, height 51 cm
Inv.no.IS61-1963
Ambikā ('Mother') is in Jainism associated with the 22nd saviour, Nemiṇātha, whose haloed image appears directly above Ambikā's,

flanked by attendants, garland bearers and celestial musicians. Ambikā is seated on a lotus throne beneath a mango tree holding a child on her lap and a mango branch in her right hand. Her vehicle (*vāhana*), the lion, is seen beneath her throne, flanked by kneeling worshippers, possibly the donors.

5

East Indian, c1120
Bodhisattva Padmapani
From a palm-leaf manuscript of
Ashtasahasrika Prajnaparamita,
7.2 × 5.8 cm
Inv.no.IS8-1958

Mughal, Rajput and British India

Northern India was dominated by Muslim sultans from the 13th century, but in 1526 the Central Asian prince Babur invaded Delhi and founded the Mughal empire. Under his grandson Akbar (ruled 1556-1605) Mughal territory expanded greatly, and imperial workshops and painting studios were established, producing great illustrated works such as the *Akbarnama*. The Emperor Jahangir (ruled 1605-27) enthusiastically embraced the naturalism introduced into India by western visitors. Painting, especially portraiture, and decorative arts flourished under Jahangir and his son Shah Jahan (ruled 1628-58). Floral designs were overwhelmingly popular and were used in all media, including architecture such as the Taj Mahal, built as a monument to Shah Jahan's wife.

The Hindu *rajas* of Western India and the Punjab Hills were strongly opposed to Mughal rule, and although they eventually succumbed to Akbar and Jahangir, their courts continued to preserve earlier Hindu traditions in their architecture and painting idioms. Many local centres developed distinctive painting styles with which to illustrate Hindu devotional and poetic texts.

European trade with India expanded from the early 17th century, and European motifs began to form an exotic element in Indian decorative design, especially in export goods such as painted cottons (chintz) from the Coromandel Coast. Hybrid styles of furniture and painting (the 'Company style') evolved through local artists working to British commissions, but other areas of Indian crafts declined during the 19th century as a result of the disappearance of court patronage.

1

1

Mughal, c1590

Emperor Akbar receives a nobleman
Gouache on paper, from a manuscript
of the *Akbarnma*; outline and painting
by Husain Naqqash, faces by Kesu;
38 × 24 cm
Inv.no.IS2-1896 (113-117)

One of the most outstanding
illustrated manuscripts produced by
Akbar's studio was the chronicle of his
reign written by his friend and
confidant Abu'l Fazl. Vigorously
naturalistic, they illustrate scenes from
the Emperor's daily life, as well as his
military campaigns and events of

state. This scene, in which Akbar
receives Husain Quli Khan Jahan,
shows the splendour of the Mughal
court at Agra.

2

4

2

Mughal, 1621

Emperor Jahangir's zebra
Gouache on paper; by Mansur;
18.3 × 24.1 cm
Inv.no.IM23-1925
In his *Memoirs*, Jahangir reveals
himself as a keen amateur naturalist,
always ready to note the peculiarities
of the flowers, birds, and animals he
encountered.

3

Rajasthan, c1525-50

The Marriage of Krishna's parents
Gouache on paper, 17.5 × 23.5 cm
Inv.no.IS1-1977
This scene of a Hindu wedding
belongs to a famous dispersed
Bhagavata Purana manuscript, narrating
events from Krishna's life. It is painted
in the bold and vivacious Early Rajput
style.

4

Mughal, c1590

Krishna's combat with Indra
Gouache on paper, from a *Harivamsa*
manuscript, 29.6 × 18.4 cm
Inv.no.IS5-1970
Unlike most Muslim rulers, Akbar was
deeply interested in the teaching of
other religions, and even initiated a
short-lived eclectic faith centred on his
own person. He also commissioned
Persian translations of the Hindu
epics, illustrated by his artists, many
of whom were themselves Hindus.
This dramatic composition shows the
aerial combat in which Krishna on the
bird Garuda overcomes Indra on his
elephant, watched from above by
other gods and celestial beings; below
is a coastal landscape scene deriving
from Flemish painting.

1
Mughal, late 16th century
Spoon
Gold, jewels, length 18.5 cm
Inv.no.IM173-1910
Surviving early examples of Mughal
jewellery and goldsmiths' work are
very rare. The shape of this gold
spoon, set with ruby and emerald
pieces and a diamond, can be related
to late 16th-century European designs.

2
Mughal, 1657
Wine-cup of Emperor Shah Jahan
Jade, dated 1657, length 18.7 cm
Inv.no.IS12-1962

3
Mughal, c1650-1700
Beaker and cover
Silver, height 14 cm
Inv.no.IS31-1961
The form of this beaker appears to
have been copied by the Mughal
craftsman from a Dutch or German
model, which had perhaps been
among the gifts presented to the
Emperor by Dutch merchants
negotiating trading rights.

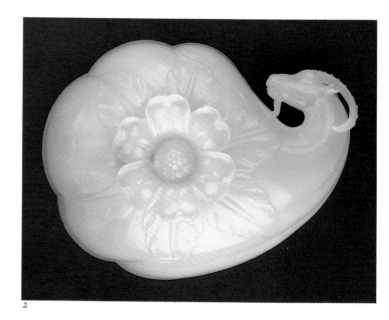
2

1

3

136

4

5

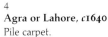

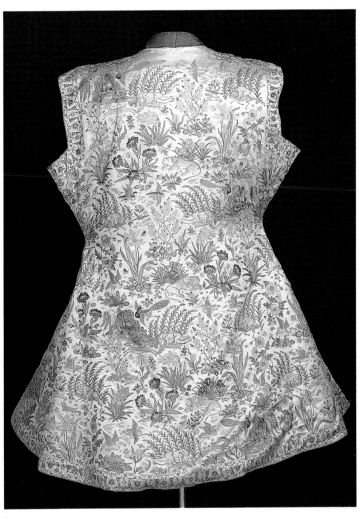

6

Agra or Lahore, *c*1640
Pile carpet.
Length 141 cm, width 90 cm
Inv.no.т403-1910
The art of pile-carpet weaving was introduced into India by Akbar, who brought craftsmen from eastern Persia to teach the skills. By the reign of Shah Jahan, when the carpet fragment was woven, the ubiquitous floral motifs found in contemporary architectural ornament, metalwork, and textiles had strongly influenced carpet design; the use of the trellis patterns suggests Italian influence.

5
Mughal, *c*1620-30
Nobleman with companions listening to music
Gouache on paper, 20 × 14.5 cm
Inv.no.is89-1965
This tranquil study of an open air music party, in which a young nobleman and companions seated under a pipal tree listen to a singer accompanied by a *tanpura* player, is an example of Mughal portraiture in its more relaxed and informal aspect.

6
Mughal, period of Jahangir (1605-27)
Satin, with embroidery, length 100 cm
Inv.no.is18-1947
This is thought to be a unique surviving example of an especially fine type of Mughal court coat referred to as *nadiri* by Jahangir in his Memoirs. Embroidered in silk chain-stitch, its pattern consists of hillocks, flowering trees and plants, peacocks, storks, ducks, butterflies, and animals, including tigers, deer, and rabbits.

1
Mughal, *c*1590

A European

Gouache on paper, 30 × 18.3 cm

Inv.no.IM386-1914

The Mughal's earliest contacts with European culture occurred when the Jesuits in Goa sent several missions to Akbar's Court in the hope of converting him to Christianity. They were followed by the representatives of the Portuguese, Dutch, and English East India Companies. This Mughal view of a European is probably based on an engraving, perhaps of the Emperor Charles V.

1

2

Golconda, _c_1640
Painted wall-hanging (detail)
Cotton, 259 × 152 cm
Inv.no.687-1898
The hand-painted and resist-dyed
cotton fabrics or chintzes of the
Coromandel coast were exported to
Europe in great numbers during the
17th and 18th centuries, and had a
profound effect on European
decorative design. They were painted
freehand in a laborious dyeing process
which imparted brilliant, non-fugitive
colours. The artists improvised from
models provided by their European
clients.

3

Sri Lankan (Kotte), _c_1540-58
The Robinson Casket
Ivory with gold fittings mounted with
sapphires, 13.7 × 22.8 × 12.7 cm
Inv.no.IS41-1980
This object belongs to a small group
of caskets which are the earliest
documented examples of Indo-
Portuguese art. It was probably
commissioned by King Dharmapala of
Kotte to accompany a diplomatic
despatch to Portugal.

4

**Gujarati (probably Ahmedabad),
early 17th century**
Travelling box
Mother-of-pearl set in black lac over a
wooden frame, 35 × 51 × 28.5 cm
Inv.no.155-1866
Travelling boxes of this type were
mentioned in 17th-century European
accounts as popular export items to
Europe.

3

4

1

Basohli, c1660-70

Resourceful Radha

Gouache on paper, 18 × 27.5 cm

Inv.no.IS48-1953

By the late 17th century, a vigorous and expressive style of manuscript illustration had become established in the Punjab Hill state of Basohli: this can be seen in the series of illustrations to the *Rasamanjari*, a Sanskrit treatise classifying ideal types of lovers and their emotions, to which this painting belongs.

2

Murshidabad, c1760-63

William Fullarton giving directions to a servant

Gouache on paper, by Dip Chand, 26.5 × 22.8 cm

Inv.no.IM33-1912

An East India Company officer sits in the attitude of a Mughal nobleman, smoking a *huqqa* on his terrace, attended by servants with yak-tail fly whisks. He is probably William Fullarton, who practised as a surgeon in Bengal and Bihar in the mid-18th century. He lived in the native quarter at Patna and while there commissioned portraits of members of his household and others from the Murshidabad artist Dip Chand.

3

Kangra, c1780

Radha and Krishna in the grove

Gouache on paper, 12.3 × 17.2 cm

Inv.no.IS15-1949

In the middle to late 18th century a remarkable final flowering of Punjab Hill painting took place, in which the technical skills brought by Mughal-trained artists returning from the plains were transformed by the poetic and devotional feeling of the Rajput tradition. At Kangra in particular, episodes from the youth of Krishna, including scenes of his love affair with Radha, were set in an idyllic version of the local landscape and rendered with rare delicacy.

4

Kotah, c1790

Maharaja Umed Singh of Kotah shooting tiger

Gouache on paper, 33 × 40 cm

Inv.no.IS563-1952

Among the various local schools of Rajasthani painting, that of Kotah was outstanding for its powerful renderings of animals and landscape, especially in hunting scenes. Raja Umed Singh and his minister Zalim Singh are seen in a tree-hide firing at the tiger which has been lured by a tethered buffalo.

1

2

3

4

141

1
'Company style' (Tanjore), c1825-30
Detail from a scroll painting
Gouache, 21.5 × 732 cm
Inv.no.IS45-1963
The British Resident is riding in a Hindu religious procession led by the Raja of Tanjore (not shown). He is followed by two local military officers.

3
Lahore or Agra, c1640
The Fremlin carpet (detail)
579 × 248 cm
Inv.no.IM1-1936
Sir Thomas Roe, the ambassador of King James I to the court of Jahangir, is known to have brought home with him 'a great carpet with my arms thereon'. His initiative was followed by other Englishmen, including William Fremlin, a prominent Company official in India, for whom this carpet was woven. Its design, mainly Persian in conception, contains mythical beasts and the Fremlin arms. It was probably used as a table-cover rather than a floor-covering, which accounts for its narrow proportions.

1

2
Mysore (Seringapatam), c1790
Tipu's tiger
Painted wood, length 177.8 cm
Inv.no.IS2545
This tiger mauling a prostrate British officer was made for Tipu Sultan, the ruler of Mysore. The tiger's body contains a miniature organ, probably of French manufacture, which ingeniously simulates its roars as well as the groans of its victim. Captured in 1799 at the fall of Seringapatam, in which Tipu himself died, it became a favourite exhibit in the East India Company's museum in London. Keats alludes to it in a satirical poem, *The Cap and Bells*.

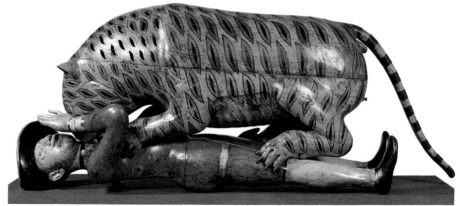

2

4

Lahore, 1818 or later
Throne of Ranjit Singh
Wood overlaid with gold, height
92 cm
Inv.no.IS2518
This impressive throne is traditionally associated with Maharaja Ranjit Singh (1780-1839), an astute and colourful ruler who united the Sikh community of the Punjab into a formidable power. The Anglo–Sikh wars which followed his death ended in the British annexation of the Punjab; the throne was brought to England and displayed in the East India Company's museum.

5

Eastern Indian (Vizagapatam), c1770
Cabinet on stand
Height 176 cm, width 104 cm, diameter 53 cm
Inv.nos.IS289-1951, IS289a-1951
Furniture made in India for the British combined European styles with local materials. The designs on two of the engraved ivory drawers on this cabinet are taken from prints of Old Montagu House, London.

3

4

5

1
Nepalese, 16th century
Torana: *Garuda attacking a naga and nagini*
Repoussé copper with gilding and paint, set with turquoise, rock crystal and semi-precious stones, height 24 cm
Inv.nos.IM142a-1926, 142b-1926

2
Nepalese, 1677
Ritual helmet
Gilt copper set with stones, dated, height 45 cm
Inv.no.IS5-1946; presented by Lt-Col E. W. A. Armstrong

Nepal and Tibet

The Himalayan region had links with Buddhism from its inception, the historical Buddha being born to a princely family at Lumbini, in southern Nepal. Buddhism was first propagated in Tibet in the 8th century and the region continued to look to India for spiritual sustenance up until the effective demise of Buddhism in India in the early 13th century. Tibetan art evolved as one aspect of a highly complex religious system combining different streams of Buddhist teachings with the indigenous animistic religion (Bon). The development of Tibetan art reflects the intense cultural interaction which occurred between Tibet and India and other neighbouring countries. Nepal, Kashmir, Central Asia and China all contributed to the evolution and character of Tibetan art.

The cultural tradition of Nepal is intimately linked to those of eastern India, as reflected in the Gupta, post-Gupta and Pala styles (4th-12th centuries AD). The production of Nepalese art was largely confined to the Newars, a Buddhist community who served Hindu and Buddhist patrons alike. This concentration of art production in one community resulted in a remarkable degree of cultural syncretism, in which Hindu and Buddhist imagery was freely appropriated to serve common religious ends. The Newars over time became the master-craftsmen of the Himalayan world, leading to a blurring of regional styles in later periods.

1

3
Tibetan, c14th century
Padmasambhava, with his wives and disciples
Gouache on prepared cotton cloth, height 58 cm
Inv.no.IS20-1970

4
Nepalese, 15th century
The Bodhisattva Amoghapasa
Gouache on cotton, 97 × 74 cm
Inv.no.IS58-1977
Amoghapasa ('He of the Infallible Noose') is a form of Avalokitesvara, the supreme *bodhisattva* of compassion. He is invoked as a saviour against natural disaster and physical torment.

5
Nepalese, 16th century
Vajradhara
Gilt copper set with turquoise, coral and lapis lazuli, height 21 cm
Inv.no.IM41-1910
Vajradhara is the embodiment of 'emptiness' or 'void', the ultimate Buddhist goal, symbolized by the *vajra* held in his right hand. The bell (*ghanta*), held in the left hand, symbolizes wisdom (*prajna*), its sound penetrating the world.

2

3

4

5

6

Nepalese, c12th century
A pair of throne legs
Ivory, height 17.5 cm
Inv.nos.IS269-1960, 269a-1960
These lions formed part of a set of
throne supports. Ivory was widely
used in India, from the earliest periods,
for luxury furniture. This pair of lions,
and a third in the British Museum,
were reportedly brought from Tibet in
1904.

1
Nepalese, 17th century
Bhairava
Repoussé copper with gilding and
paint, set with turquoise, rock crystal
and semi-precious stones, height
69.2 cm
Inv.no.IM172-1913

2
Nepalese early 15th century
Temple Banner
Silk embroidered on cotton,
40.5 × 32 cm
Inv.no.IS6-1989

3
Nepalese, c14th-early 15th century
The bodhisattva Avalokiteśvara
Gilt copper with inset precious and
semi-precious stones, height 91.5 cm
Inv.no.IM239-1922
The *bodhisattva* stands in the relaxed
'three bends' (*tribhaṅga*) posture, his
right hand lowered in the gesture of
granting wishes or favours
(*varadamudrā*).

1

2

3

South-East Asia

The region identified as South-East Asia was known to the early geographer Ptolemy (2nd century AD) as the 'India beyond the Ganges'. The early history of the region is dominated by the influx of ideas from India on social organization, kingship and religion. This was essentially Sanskritic Brahmanical culture which was absorbed by the ruling elite and priest class, providing a cultural framework and apparatus for developing notions of kingship and state formation. India provided the framework upon which the local cultures were able to elaborate, integrating indigenous traditions and beliefs with imported concepts and models. The artistic legacy of Angkor in Kampuchea, Pagan in Burma, Sukhothai in Thailand and the temple complexes of central and east Java demonstrate the extent to which Indian culture penetrated these kingdoms.

The early sculptures of South-East Asia reveal the widespread practise of Indian cults, particularly those associated with Śiva, Vishnu and Harihara. Buddhism, particularly Mahayana, also prospered, although Hinduism appears to have been favoured by most rulers. The later revival of Hinayana Buddhism, as practised in Burma and Thailand today, owes much to the missionary activity of Sri Lankan monks, who were widely revered as the protectors of 'original' Buddhism. South-East Asia gained much of its wealth from trade, serving the great East-West trade routes which linked China with the Arab world and the West. Islamic and Chinese influences, transmitted both through trade and settlement, made important contributions to the region's cultural complexion, especially in the later periods.

1
Mon, Dvaravati kingdom, *c*7th-8th century
Head of the Buddha
Sandstone, height 26.5 cm
Inv.no.IS140-1961
The head is from a freestanding image of the Buddha. Images of the Buddha were produced in considerable quantities under Dvaravati patronage in central and southern Thailand, both as monumental cult images and, like this example, to decorate architecture. Standing Buddhas were positioned in architectural niches, in the manner continued in later Thai temple decoration.

2

1

3

2
Thai (Lopburi), 13th century
Head of the Buddha
Sandstone, height 38.5 cm
Inv.no.IM62-1927
This sculpture reflects the emergence of a distinct Thai style at Lopburi in the 13th century. It is clearly based on Khmer conventions, particularly those of the Bayon, the late 12th century monument at Angkor which set the style for the last phase of Khmer art.

3
Burmese, Pagan period, 12th century
Scenes from the life of the Buddha
Steatite, height 8.5 cm
Inv.no.IM378-1914
This subject is known from a number of examples found at Pagan and dates from the Pagan period (11th-13th century). It is based on contemporary eastern Indian models of the Pala school. The central figure of the Buddha, raised on a lotus seat (*padmasana*), is surrounded by seven subsidiary scenes, illustrating significant events in the Buddha's life.

1

Thai (Si Satchonalai), 15th century
Jar
Celadon glaze, height 16.3 cm
Inv.no.c238-1927
Stoneware ceramics were made in
central Thailand during this period
and large quantities were exported
throughout South-East Asia.

1

2

3

4

2
Burmese, 19th century
Container in the form of a sacred bird
Gold, set with rubies and imitation
emeralds, height 45.5 cm
Inv.nos.IS246-1964, 246a-1964;
presented by the Government of the
Union of Burma in generous
recognition of the Victoria & Albert
Museum's safekeeping of the
Mandalay Regalia (1886-1964).

3
Burmese (Pegu), late 15th century
Tile: *The Warriors of Mara*
Glazed stoneware, height 47.5 cm
Inv.no.IS2-1966
Built by the pious King Dhammaceti
in 1476 to honour the life of the
Buddha.

4
Burmese, late 19th century
Puppet figure
Carved and painted wood, with
costume of silk embroidered with gold
thread, sequins, pieces of mirror, and
glass beads, height 63.5 cm
Inv.no.IS33-1966
Puppet shows were patronized by the
Burmese kings, and an official at court
was in charge of performances. The
themes of the plays were taken from
the stories of Buddha's previous
births, and incidents in Burmese
history. As well as providing
entertainment, they had a moral
element, such as the triumph of virtue
over vice, and included
extemporizations which were used as
outlets for comment on current affairs.

5
Burmese, late 19th century
Illustration from a folding book
Gouache in paper, height 20 cm
Inv.no.IS8-1955
Usually of a religious nature, Burmese
painting consists of wall-paintings or
illustrations to texts. This book
illustration shows a disciple of the
Buddha seated with a king in his
palace, and also flying with the king's
gift for the Buddha. The illustrations
are simple and direct and a highly
decorative effect is achieved by using
bright colours and gold paint.

6
Burmese, c1910-20
Bowl
Lacquer, height 34 cm
Inv.no.IM57-1932
Lacquer was used in making shrines
and images, it was also employed in
the manufacture of book pages and
covers, headdresses, musical
instruments, furniture, architectural
details, and boxes and bowls such as
the one illustrated here.

5

6

1

Burmese, late 19th century
Sword (*dha*)
Mounts of gold and spinel rubies,
length 94 cm
Inv.no.IS2574
There are several types of *dha*, from
those used for clearing undergrowth
to efficient weapons of self-defence.

This one is similar to the latter type
but was intended more for ceremonial
use than for battle. Its sumptuous
decoration lends support to the
tradition that it was given by King
Mindon of Burma to Lord Dalhousie
(Governor-General of India) in about
1854.

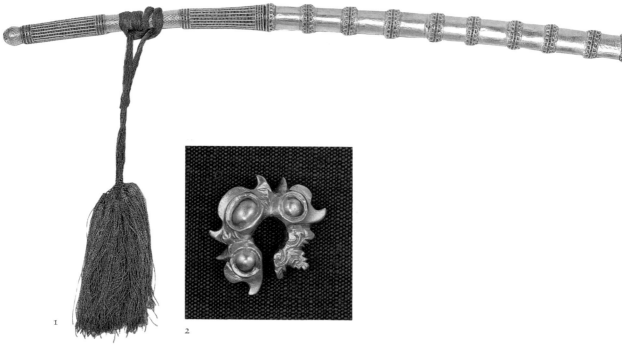

1

2

2

East Javanese, 13th–15th century
Ear ornament
Gold, height 2.5 cm
Inv.no.IS15-1978
Earrings are among the most popular
forms of Javanese jewellery, and are
made in a great variety of shapes. The
one shown here is in the shape of a
mythological bird.

2

Javanese, late 19th century
Skirt cloth (Lain panjang)
Woven silk with batik pattern,
256.5 × 109 cm
Inv.no.IM265-1921
Java has used the technique of batik
for at least two hundred years, during
which time many beautiful patterns
have been produced. They have
strong, lively, designs which often
combine foliage and geometrical
motifs executed in harmonious colours. A slight crackle, caused by the
partial breaking of the wax resist,
sometimes adds to their attraction.
There are many versions of this one,
which was originally only worn by
persons of princely rank.

3

The Islamic Collections

The faith of Islam is centred on the revelations received by the Arab Prophet Muhammed in the early 7th century, later recorded in the Quran. During his lifetime, Muhammed succeeded in uniting the various nomadic Arab tribes of the Saudi Arabian peninsular under the banner of Islam, and from the holy cities of Mecca and Medina built the foundations of a new social order. Soon after his death in AD 632 the Islamic armies erupted from the peninsular to conquer Syria and Egypt, the richest provinces of the Byzantine Empire, and to destroy the Sasanian Empire of Iraq and Iran. Other conquests followed which established the rule of Islam from Central Asia in the east to North Africa and Spain in the west. Though political control soon fragmented, the religion and culture of Islam assured a unity and coherence among many different peoples widely spread across the globe – and Islam to this day remains a major cultural and political world force.

Despite diverse origins, the arts of the Near East gradually evolved many features in common that can only be called Islamic. The mosque itself is a leading example, deriving its architectural layout from its role as a Muslim house of prayer, and remaining always orientated both physically and metaphorically towards Mecca. Its interior furnishings show to Western eyes a characteristic simplicity which springs from the religious disapproval of the depiction of human or animal form for fear of idolatry and the blasphemy of attempting to rival the creative powers of God. The effects of this rejection are less strongly felt in the secular arts of Islam, where humans and animals often play an important decorative role. The architecture of the mosque was complemented in other ways: by the rich texture and colour of carpets, intricately carved and inlaid woodwork, and sumptuously tiled walls; and these and other crafts achieved an unrivalled development of pattern and design in which plant and geometrical motifs are woven together in infinitely subtle variations of arabesque, interlace, and scrollwork. However, the most important means of spreading the message of the Quran was the written word, and thus the art of calligraphy took on a special status, and inscriptions in a wide variety of scripts came to be everywhere a prominent feature in design. In a very real sense it is Arabic – the language of God – which gives Islamic art much of its identity and character.

In comparison with Christianity and with Hinduism or other Eastern religions, Islam has few requirements for specifically 'religious' objects. The Quran – the Islamic holy book – is the most important religious object. Among the necessary

furnishings of the Mosque is the *minbar* – a pulpit in the form of a staircase from which the weekly Friday sermon is delivered. Other mosque furnishings include carpets and lamps of metal or glass.

Most Islamic art objects are purely functional. The carpets are the main furnishing of houses which contain little other furniture in a European sense. Textiles were much used as hangings and coverings as well as for clothes. The ceramics, glass and metalwork were used in the preparation and serving of food and drink or for other household tasks. Very few objects are purely decorative, though luxury objects all tend to be highly decorated. Even painting predominantly serves as the illustration to books in which the calligraphy was often more highly regarded.

From the earliest times, the manufacture of textiles formed the largest and most varied industry. Clothes, carpets and coverings would have formed the wealthy Muslim's most significant possessions. Because of their fragile nature, early textiles generally survive only as faded scraps; it is not until fairly recent times that one can begin to experience and understand the dominant role that luxury textiles played, and the enormous impact they made. In a similar way, the extraordinary pomp and richness of court life in the Islamic capitals is only hinted at by the few rare surviving examples of luxury objects such as carved ivory boxes, or the extraordinary jug carved from a single block of rock-crystal.

Certain other ancient crafts also underwent major changes within Islamic culture. Pottery, for example, broke new ground to become a luxury possession for the burgeoning urban middle classes. Islamic inventions were sometimes sparked by a desire to match imports of porcelain from China, but much local inventiveness is manifest. New white-glazed wares, first developed to imitate porcelains, are decorated in colours, and especially in a new golden lustre pigment, in which animals and humans are depicted in lively fashion. A purely Islamic technique is the bold use of contrasting coloured slips with painted or carved designs, while Islamic potters may be credited with the independent invention of such important techniques as enamel- and underglaze-painting. Resplendent colour is everywhere, and never to more effect than in the extensive glazed tilework now used to decorate the walls of mosques and palaces and baths. Metalworkers perfected the art of cast and inlaid design in which functional vessels of bronze and brass are highly elaborated with details in gold and silver.

1
Turkish (Iznik), c1545
Footed bowl
White earthenware with underglaze
painted decoration, height 42.6 cm
Inv.no.243-1876

In the late 15th century, there
developed at Iznik the production of
some of the highest quality pottery
seen in the Islamic world. The spiral
decoration of this impressive large
bowl is derived from contemporary
manuscript illumination.

1

2

3

2
Egyptian, c1100-50
Bowl
White glazed earthenware with lustre
decoration, diameter 30.8 cm
Inv.no.c49-1952
The image depicts a Christian Coptic
priest carrying a lamp or censer. Large

Christian and Jewish communities
remained under Islamic rule, with the
special status of 'peoples of the book',
ie those who recognised essentially
the same God, but who believed in
earlier, and to Muslims misguided,
versions of the same religion.

3
Egyptian, *c*1000
Ewer
Rock crystal, height 21.6 cm
Inv.no.7904-1862
This ewer is of the highest luxury and
of breathtaking skill. The whole
object, including the handle, is carved
from a single block of rock-crystal. It
would have been used to serve wine
or other drink at the court of the
Egyptian Fatimid dynasty, and it
eventually found its way into a
Spanish cathedral treasury.

4
Iraqi, *c*1200
Jar
White earthenware with underglaze-
painting, height 26.7 cm
Inv.no.c137-1929
The sweeping curves of the
calligraphy in the main decorative
band are answered by the elegant
floral sprays in the lower part.

4

1

West Persian, 13th century
Ewer
Brass inlaid with silver and gold,
height 37.8 cm
Inv.no.381-1897

2

2

Persian, 1207
Dish
White earthenware with lustre
decoration, diameter 34.9 cm
Inv.no.c51-1952
The horserider is playing polo – a
courtly sport in mediaeval Persia.

3

3
Egyptian, *c*1300
Candlestick
Bronze inlaid with silver, height
35.8 cm
Inv.no.M716-1910
This is a standard form of candlestick
used over many centuries in the
Islamic world.

4
Central Asian (Bukhara), *c*1360
Calligraphic frieze
Carved earthenware with coloured
glazes, height 23.5 cm
Inv.no.2013a-1899
The tiles formed part of the
decoration of the tomb of a certain
Buyan Kuli Khan.

5
Syrian, 14th century
Pottery jar, height 38.1 cm
Inv.no.483-1864
Bold design is a feature of these
Syrian wares which are painted in blue
and black under a thick, glassy glaze
with birds and debased calligraphic
motifs.

4

5

6

6
Syrian, mid-13th century
Goblet, 'The Luck of Edenhall'
Glass with enamelled decoration,
height 15.9 cm
Inv.no.C1-1959
Furnished with a case of French
stamped-leather of the 14th century,
this famous glass was possibly
brought from the Holy Lands by a
crusader on his return.

Persian, 1539
The 'Ardabil' carpet
Woollen pile on a silk weft,
1097 × 534 cm
Inv.no.272-1893
Possibly the world's most famous
carpet, this magnificent piece is one of
a pair said to have been formerly at
Ardabil, the ancestral shrine of the
Safavid dynasty that ruled Iran during
the 16th and 17th century. Enormous
in size, it bears the name of Maqsud of
Kashan, probably the weaver. The
design follows a pattern that is found
also on book-bindings, illuminations
and other decorative arts of the
period.

2

Persian, c1430
*Shah Rukh defeats Pir Padishah of
Khurasan*
Illustration from the historical text of
Hafiz-i Abru, height 17.8 cm
Inv.no.E5499-1958
The illustration is unusual for Persian
miniature painting in that it depicts a
real historical event that took place
only 25 years previously. It depicts, in
the realistic yet stylized manner
typical of Persian book illustration, a
victory by the ruler who
commissioned the text.

3

Persian, c1600
Dish of so-called 'Kubachi' ware
White earthenware with underglaze
painted decoration, diameter 34.6 cm
Inv.no.c58-1952
Considerably inferior in quality to
Turkish Iznik wares from which they
derived a certain inspiration, the
Kubachi ceramics from North West
Iran nevertheless show all the subtlety
and grace of line of contemporary
Persian miniature painting.

1

4

Persian, 16th century
The 'Chelsea' carpet
Woollen pile on a silk warp,
539 × 295 cm
Inv.no.589-1890

The 'Chelsea' carpet is one of the best
preserved and most elaborate of
classical Persian carpets of the 16th
century. Its very high quality is shown
by the fine knotting, the wide range of
colours and the skill of drawing the
intricate motifs.

2

4

3

1

Persian, 1632

Khusrau and the lion

Illustration to the romance of *Khusrau and Shirin* by Nizami, painted by Riza Abbasi, 26.7 × 15.3 cm

Inv.no.L1613-1964

In the 19th century this painting was detached from the manuscript (which the Museum also owns) and mounted, in European style, as a separate image. The style of drawing, notwithstanding the dramatic event that it portrays, shows the soft and sensual lines characteristic of the period during which Riza Abbasi was the acknowledged master.

5

6

2
Persian, c1600
Tile panel
White earthenware with coloured-glaze painted decoration, height 109.3 cm
Inv.no.139-1891
This tile panel would have decorated one of the royal pavilions in the gardens at Isfahan, the capital of the Safavid dynasty, where activities like those depicted on the tiles took place.

3
Persian, 17th century
Dish
White earthenware with blue underglaze painting, diameter 27.5 cm
Inv.no.1153-1876
Much late Persian pottery consists of close copies after Chinese blue-and-

white porcelains which were exported in large quantities to the Middle East. The drawing shows a charmingly naive rendering of the original Chinese design.

4
Turkish, c1500
Helmet
Iron inlaid with silver, height 35.5 cm
Inv.no.399-1888

5
Persian, c1600
Length of cloth
Velvet with silver on a gold ground, 160 × 76 cm
Inv.no.T226-1923
This length, possibly used as a decorative hanging or intended to be cut for a coat, represents the highest

quality of luxury textile of the period. The opulence of the technique is matched by the sensual and languorous drawing of the figures typical of the period.

6
Persian, 16th-17th century
Length of cloth
Brocaded silk, 176 × 110 cm
Inv.no.T9-1915
This cloth would probably have been used as a wall-hanging, possibly to decorate a tent or other outdoor shelter during ceremonies or festivities. The formal palmette design is enlivened by a pair of hovering butterflies.

Index